A BIBLICAL FAITH FOR
THE AGE OF SCIENCE

A BIBLICAL FAITH FOR THE AGE OF SCIENCE

EUGENE WAGNER

Copyright © 2005 by Eugene Wagner.

Illustrated by the author

Library of Congress Number   2004096949

ISBN :   Hardcover   1-4134-6650-8

                Softcover   1-4134-6649-4

This book was printed in the United States of America.

To order additional copies of this book, contact:
Xlibris Corporation
1-888-795-4274
www.Xlibris.com
Orders@Xlibris.com
26447

CONTENTS

Introduction 9

PART I: THE FACTS OF LIFE

Chapter One: In the Beginning 23

Chapter Two: Evolution is not a Four–Letter Word 41

Chapter Three: You Animal, You 59

Chapter Four: Why Suffering? 73

Chapter Five: More than Human 83

Chapter Six: The God of Chance 100

Chapter Seven: Science, the Brain, and the Soul 115

Chapter Eight: The Reality of Jesus 127

PART II: OUT OF THIS WORLD

Chapter Nine: Where is God? 141

Chapter Ten: Is Anyone Else Out There? 153

The Last Word 165

Books Cited 167

To my wife, Betty, to Amy, Paul, Eric,
Tasha and Madison and to my mother, Dorothy

INTRODUCTION

Is it possible to believe in the Bible and still appreciate the fantastic discoveries that science has made and will continue to make? I believe, as do many theologians today, that such a Bible-and-science-based theology is not only possible but even necessary in this modern age. In 1988, Pope John Paul II wrote that science "can purify religion from error and superstition," and religion "can purify science from idolatry and false absolutes." In this book, I hope to show that not only can we believe in both the Bible and science, but that science can add to our understanding of the Bible. Science today has a lot to say to the interpretation of scripture, and some very difficult problems that the theologians have struggled with for centuries are now beginning to find an explanation in the discoveries of modern science. It's a journey worth taking, both for the joy of it and for the foundation it can give to your faith. Without this synthesis, you will have a faith built on sand that could be severely shaken by the next scientific discovery. It is far better to have your faith built on the solid rock of compatible truth, where science no longer poses a threat to faith but becomes an additional means of God's revelation.

To consider the study of the universe by science to be a revelation of God's truth is, after all, essentially what Paul was talking about in Romans 1:20*a*.

> Ever since God created the world, his invisible qualities, both his eternal power and his divine nature, have been clearly seen; they are perceived in the things that God has made. (TEV)

If as Christians, we believe that God created all that exists in the physical world, and science is the study of that physical world, then God's eternal nature and glory should be revealed to us in the discoveries of science. The fact is, this is even more true today than it was in Paul's time. The discoveries of modern science have revealed things in the natural world unimaginable to first-century Christians. Today, we can see and speak in an instant with someone on the other side of the globe or even visit them in just a few hours. We can watch as a spacecraft soars through the glittering rings of the planet Saturn or view the pulsing of life in the tiniest cell. We can scan a rusty, arid landscape on Mars or visit strange creatures living in the dark depths of the Atlantic Ocean rift. The very heart of the atom and the edge of the universe are open to us. How much more magnificent does God's power and deity appear when we contemplate the enormity of the universe and the simplicity of the laws that govern it. The discoveries of science present us with an unending treasure for the soul in the revealed beauty of God's creation—a treasure that no other generation before us has had the blessing to know.

Today science has reached a level of understanding of the universe that brings it into the realm of the unobservable, whether it is in the study of the earliest moments of creation, the farthest reaches of space probed by our strongest telescopes, or the smallest particles of matter smashed to bits in giant accelerators. These are points at which science becomes impotent to observe and understand further. As these limits are approached, some scientists are realizing what the theologians have known all along—that there must be a great intelligence and power behind all that exists, a great creative force that is God.

In John 8:32, Jesus promised,

> You will know the truth, and the truth will set you free. (TEV)

Indeed, the truths revealed by science can free us from superstition and fear. By better understanding of the natural world, we have eliminated the fear of such things as eclipses and meteors. No longer does modern man see the anger of the gods in the volcano or the storm. Only a few people really believe that the configuration of the stars and planets at our birth has anything to do with what will happen in our lives. Although there are many things in the natural world that still threaten us, including our own misuse of the planet, we now see them as problems to be solved with study and logic rather than by incantation and sacrifice. Truth about the physical universe has freed us to lead healthier, more productive, and more meaningful lives.

Undoubtedly, Jesus was also talking about another kind of truth. If he had any purpose in his life, it was to reveal to us the importance of the truth of the spiritual universe. To Jesus, the spiritual universe is the realm of God and, therefore, the fundamental source of life and all that exists. If we know the truth of the spiritual universe, as well as the truth of the physical universe, we are in touch with the ultimate power and reality of existence. God in his infinite wisdom has given us two methods to seek truth, each designed to discover truth in one of the two realities—*the universe of spiritual reality and the universe of physical reality.* These two realities represent the two aspects which our existence presents to us. We can only know the truth of the spiritual universe by *faith* and the truth of the physical universe by *science.* The two methods are not the same because the two universes are not the same, but since they seek to know different aspects of the same creation, they must be complementary. Only by using both methods together can we have any hope of experiencing the truth of the entire universe in which we live.

American history shows some examples of the combination of science (and technology) and faith working together to further God's revelation to us. The scientific study of genetics showed that the African slaves were of the same species as their white owners because they could mate and produce offspring (something the slave-owners took advantage of). This refuted the concept that they were animals to be bought and sold like cattle. Coupled with the Judeo-Christian concept of the equality and importance of each person to God, science and Christianity worked together to provide the rationale necessary to abolish slavery in this country and the world. Likewise, science and technology have given us the machinery of the industrial age, to improve our lives, both in the jobs we do and in the lives we lead. However, initially, the industrial age led to shameful abuse of people in unsafe factories with demeaning wages. But people armed with the Christian moral concept of the worth of the individual forced the improvement of the conditions and the protection of the workers. And in spite of a commonly held view that Christianity is antiwomen, Christ was the actually the first to liberate them to a status of equality and importance. When science and technology finally liberated much household drudgery, the modern women began to claim their rightful place as full partners with men in the modern world. With science and faith together, the revelation continues.

Unfortunately, science and faith don't always work together. Some of our industrial and governmental decisions seem to demonstrate the consequences of the failure to use the knowledge derived from both faith and science. When our health care system seemed to put an emphasis on the human fear of disease with no concern for cost, it nearly drove us to bankruptcy. Today, our health care system seems to have failed to put human needs into the equation and it is now driven by cost. We need people of faith and science to find the balance that will continue to give us the best care. An understanding of both faith and science is essential.

The church must share some of the blame for the widely acknowledged scientific ignorance in our society today. Because of this lack of understanding of the role of science in God's revelation, and because science threatens certain beliefs taken from the Bible, some churches have discouraged their followers from studying science, or have even distorted science to make it conform to their faith. The so-called creationists are the most vocal such group. The ignorance and fear of science is all the more tragic since scientifically informed Christians are necessary to help us develop moral solutions to the technical problems that arise in society. Indeed, without Judeo-Christian moral values, we have social decisions made on cost, greed, or simply politics. Without scientific knowledge, we have decisions based on superstition, ignorance, or fear.

The scientific community must also share some of the burden for this lack of mutual trust between the church and science. Too often when scientists present themselves as the only source of truth in the world, people of faith stop listening. This misled scientific self-confidence comes from the very nature of science itself and how it views truth. Science deals in facts that can be proven by experiment. Since science is incapable of experimenting on God, God can't be defined scientifically. Yet some scientists claim that God cannot exist, even though they must know that absence of proof is no proof of absence. Certainly, such arrogance doesn't encourage church-science understanding.

Another problem is that science is continually changing. What was once thought to be right is now shown to be wrong. This gives many people the excuse not to accept any of it, especially that which challenges their beliefs. But science delights in new knowledge and better understanding, because often great new progress can be made as theory moves closer to fact. In contrast, when new truth comes to religion, a messiah is crucified, heretics are burned, churches are divided, and faith is lost. As superstition and religious interpretations of natural phenomena have been refuted and destroyed by scientific scrutiny, religion has retreated, cursing science in the process rather than blessing it for rescuing the faith from misunderstanding and untruth.

So it is important at this point to understand just what science is and what it is not. *Science is simply knowledge of the physical world and the search for that knowledge.* It definitely is not something to idolize as the only way to all truth, as some scientists claim. They have faith in science alone and only in what can be observed and determined by experiment. Science is only a method. By its very nature, science is limited to the study of that which can be observed and tested. It is hostage to experimentation. Science, through observation, experimentation, deduction, correlation, comparison, hypothesis, and theory, seeks to discover truth about the physical world. *Technology is the application of scientific knowledge to practical use.* We must remember that science and technology are gifts from God to help us better fulfill the command given us in Genesis

1:27-28 to have responsibility for the earth. For instance, where once we could only scratch out a meager existence from the soil, we now can feed millions thanks to the discoveries of agricultural science and technology. Where it once took several days to travel from Boston to New York, such a trip now takes minutes. The power of scientific knowledge and technology for good in this world is great, for Jesus said that God does not give us bad gifts:

> As bad as you are, you know how to give good things to
> your children. How much more, then, will your Father
> in heaven give good things to those who ask him!
> (Matthew 7:11)(TEV)

Indeed, it is by God's providence that the scientific method works. It is his will that the world is discernible, verifiable, and scientifically rational. Einstein was reported to have marveled that the universe was knowable at all. Without God's providence, science would be impossible. The universe must be consistent and reliable. God does not change his laws at whim just to play tricks on us or confuse us. If that were so, we would still be in the Stone Age, impotent to improve our lot. It has even been suggested that the reason why science has flourished in Europe after the Middle Ages, and not in the great civilizations of antiquity, is that the Judeo-Christian belief in an omnipotent God gives us our basic concept that history is moving forward and that the order of the universe is accessible to the human mind. In fact, many of the early scientists were men of the church.

Scientific facts must then be consistent with God's truth, for all truth emanates from the same source. The facts of the physical universe are interpretable from a Christian perspective, and the facts of the Christian faith are interpretable from a scientific perspective. As the fictional theologian, Palmer Joss, in the late Carl Sagan's novel *Contact,* said,

> There were many interpretations of scripture and many
> interpretations of the natural world. Both were created by

God, so both must be mutually consistent. Whenever a discrepancy seems to exist, either a scientist or a theologian—maybe both—hasn't been doing his job.

Science, after all, is limited to a study of the physical world. Science cannot prove nor can it disprove God, for it is incapable of observing anything that is not of the physical world. Although we can discern some of God's attributes, his majesty, power, and deity, by observing the physical universe, we cannot prove that God exists by human logic, experimentation, or study. As was asked in the book of Job:

> Can you fathom the mysteries of God? Can you probe the limits of the Almighty? They are higher than the heavens—what can you do? They are deeper than the depths of the grave—what can you know? (Job 11:7-8)(NIV)

Jesus said that God is a spirit (John 4:24), and therefore, beyond human ability to study him. In fact, the Creator God of the universe deliberately chose not to be provable by his creation's efforts and brain power.

> For God in his wisdom made it impossible for people to know him by means of their own wisdom. (1 Corinthians 1:21)(TEV)

If this were not so, only the wise or scholarly, only the scientist, could come to God and know him. Instead, God can only be *known* by faith. We can *know about* God from study of the universe around us, but only faith will let us have a relationship with him. Polls have said that 95 percent of the American people believe there is a God, but they do not all have faith. Faith, after all, is not just belief in God or that God exists. *Faith is living our belief in trust and obedience,* and having such a faith gives us the understanding that is described in Hebrews:

To have faith is to be sure of the things we hope for, to be
certain of the things we cannot see. It was by their faith that
people of ancient times won God's approval.

It is by faith that we understand that the universe was
created by God's word, so that what can be seen was made
out of what cannot be seen. (Hebrews 11:1-3)(TEV)

The Error of Creationism

I will not spend much time in this book refuting *creationism*.
But it is so loudly proclaimed in the press and among
fundamentalist Protestant groups in this country that the average
Christian must take notice. For Christians dedicated to the Bible
as God's word, it is an easy trap to fall into. It is an error that is as
slippery and seductive as the snake's temptation of Eve. Creationism
is fundamentally a belief that God created the world. Indeed, I am
a creationist if it means someone who believes that God was the
creator of the universe. But creationists, often erroneously calling
themselves "scientific creationists," insist on more than that. They
attempt to force the facts of science to conform to a literal
interpretation of the Bible. And there I have to part company
with them. Creationism is seriously flawed because it is false
science.

Unfortunately, those people espousing creationism, although
claiming to be Christians and defenders of the faith, are using
falsehoods and misrepresentations to promote their agenda. A recent
example where a creationist proclaimed that the late Harvard
professor Stephen J. Gould, "devout evolutionist, author, and
lecturer," admitted that traditional Darwinian evolution is dead.
The creationist was using as a refutation of evolution Gould's idea
that Darwin's concept of evolution has undergone considerable
refinement since Darwin's day. But later Gould wrote that evolution
was so well proven that Christians need to accept it as fact and not
just as a possibility.

Does that sound like a man who has thrown out the idea of
evolution? I think not. Yet the creationists, in their determination

to force science to conform to their literal interpretation of the Bible, have continually misrepresented scientists and scientific facts to suit their own purposes. And what they cannot win by logic and fact, they try to obtain by politics. The publicity given to their efforts to control the teaching of evolution in the schools has been a case in point. These people, though discredited in the courts, will not go away. And they still have strong influence in the many Christian schools. The "creationism movement" is flawed because it forces preconceived ideas upon the scientific data. Scientists must constantly fight the temptation to look at their results with preconceived ideas, because that is a certain road to disaster. Creationism is also false because it is based on biblical literalism which insists on the absolute accuracy (both spiritual and scientific) of the Bible.

The Error of Literalism

For the literalist, the Bible was written by God, with man's hand holding the pen. However, nowhere in the Bible does it claim to be dictated by God. Rather, it clearly indicates that it was written by many authors, all of whom were "inspired" by God, not dictated to. If God had dictated it, why do we have four versions of the Gospel—Matthew, Mark, Luke, and John—all of which have differences in the description of some events? Some differences are marked, such as Jesus cleansing the temple in his last week in the first three Gospels and in his early ministry in the Gospel of John. If God had written it, you would have thought he would have gotten it right the first time. As Vernon Robbins of Chandler School of Theology in Atlanta is reported to have said, "The words of the Bible are not themselves the Word of God. They are human language that is presenting the Word of God."

The Bible is obviously a record of a people's relationship to God, his revelation to them, and his love for them. These ancient people were not scientists in the modern sense. They did not write a book about science; they wrote a book about God. If their science is shaky, their awareness of God was not.

The literalists insist that if you don't accept everything in the Bible as absolutely true, then all of it is suspect and you really don't believe any of it. But that is a specious argument. The Bible is, after all, a library of books written over many hundreds of years by many authors. The logic of rejecting it all if a word is untrue would require that we do not accept any book in the public library as true since some of the books are fiction. Would we be willing to totally destroy all fiction because it does not speak accurately of life? Of course not. Fiction often presents the most precise description of the meaning of life that we have. It is likely that the originators of some of these biblical stories understood that they were only stories. That is clearly demonstrated by the fact that there are two completely different and incompatible creation stories. The compilers of the Old Testament were not afraid of this because both stories had something to say about God. In addition, it is of the Eastern Mediterranean thought pattern to wrap philosophical concepts in a story. Some obvious examples of such tales are the Garden of Eden, the Tower of Babel, Noah's Ark, Jonah and the Whale, and Balaam and the Donkey. But once these stories became part of the Bible, they were enveloped in its aura of truth. These stories are true, not because the events are true, but because they tell us something about God acting in people's lives. If we refused to allow such stories in the Bible, then Jesus must be denied the Prodigal Son and the Good Samaritan and all his other parables. If some of the stories in the Bible are fiction, that in no way denigrates what they tell us about God.

Actually, there are many items in the Bible that even the most inflexible literalists don't really accept as true. In Genesis 6:4 it says,

> The Nephilim [giants] were on the earth in those days—
> and also afterward—when the sons of God went in to the
> daughters of humans, who bore children to them. These
> were the heroes that were of old, warriors of renown. (NRSV)

If that is true, then so is all of Greek mythology. When they are faced with such things, literalists will try to find an explanation for it by reinterpreting its meaning or giving it a "spiritual" meaning. But having to reinterpret its meaning means that they are not accepting the literal truth of the Bible, and a crack has just appeared in the wall of absolutism that they force, unfairly and unreasonably, upon the Bible.

I sincerely believe we must look at the Bible at face value and accept it for what it is, not what we wish it to be. My proposal is that we let the Bible be the Bible and science be science. It is our task as Christians to make sense of them both for they both will glorify God.

God has given us science to be our best source of knowledge about the physical universe. The Bible is still our best source of knowledge about God, faith, and life in the spiritual universe. Jesus promised us that the truth will free us and this applies to our knowledge of both realities. The truth revealed by science frees us from superstition and ignorance and gives access to the power of the physical universe. The truth revealed by Christianity frees us from total dependence upon the physical universe and gives us access to the power of the spiritual universe. Both truths are vital to becoming a true citizen of the whole of reality—both universes—the seen and the unseen.

What follows is, of course, my statement of faith as a Christian and as a scientist. I share it with you that your faith may be built on the rock, no longer threatened by scientific discoveries, but that these may be seen as a continuation of God's revelation to us. I also share it so that your knowledge of the world might be infused with an understanding that the physical universe was created out of the more powerful spiritual universe—the universe which is the ultimate goal of our existence.

PART I

THE FACTS OF LIFE

Christians need to know the truth
about the birds and the bees—
and all the rest of God's creation

CHAPTER ONE

IN THE BEGINNING

By the word of the Lord the heavens were made, and all their
host by the breath of his mouth.
He gathered the waters of the sea as in a bottle; he put the deeps
in storehouses.
Let all the earth fear the Lord, let all the inhabitants of the
world stand in awe of him.
For he spoke, and it came to be; he commanded, and it stood firm.
(Psalm 33:6-9)(NRSV)

There is no place of greater conflict between science and
Christianity than "in the beginning." Those Christians who believe
the Bible is the inerrant Word of God are forced to accept the
ancient creation stories of Genesis as total fact, and all of natural
science must therefore be in error since it does not conform to
those stories. Indeed, natural science tells quite a different story
from what the Bible says, and on the surface, agreement doesn't
seem possible. I will attempt to show you that when we face up to
exactly what these creation stories are and what they say,
understanding them in relationship to modern scientific theory
becomes no problem at all. It is as futile to attempt to force the
stories to fit modern science or make them into allegories as it is to
force modern science to fit the stories. We must accept them for
what they are: ancient concepts of creation. When we approach
them on their own terms, anyone, even an atheist, will see that
they are beautiful and, for their time, very revolutionary. That is
sufficient to confirm that they were God inspired (which doesn't

mean God-written). They don't have to conform to modern scientific theory. They are there to tell us something about our Creator God, and what they reveal to us is still valid today.

As we begin we must consider three facts about the creation stories in the Bible that almost all scholars of the Bible would agree upon.

1. **There are two different stories:** The first runs from Genesis 1:1-2:4*a* and consists of the seven days of creation. The second in Genesis 2:4*b*-4:26 tells of Adam and Eve in the Garden of Eden. (The chapter divisions were made much later and do not, in this case, correlate with the story.) A different authorship is suggested by the fact that a different Hebrew name for God is used in each. Although the two stories have been juxtaposed, they were not edited by the biblical compilers to make them fit into a single logical narrative.

2. **They were written over 2,000 years ago.** Biblical scholar Julius Wellhausen determined in the nineteenth century that the first was probably written down in the sixth century BC and the second, even older, was written in the ninth century BC. They were presumably derived from earlier oral traditions and they have strong ties to Mesopotamian creation myths.

3. **The exact mode of creation is not an essential doctrine to Christianity.** Creation is discussed in the New Testament, only figuratively in the opening to the Gospel of John, and when Paul compares Christ with Adam in 1 Corinthians 15. John indicates that Jesus was also involved in creation as a part of the Godhead, but belief in the details of the creation stories is never required for salvation, either in the Old or the New Testament.

The creation stories in Genesis contain many parallels with the ancient Assyrian creation epics found in the library of Assyrian king Asshurbanapal (668-627 BC) where archeologists in the nineteenth century discovered thousands of tablets covering all aspects of Assyrian life and knowledge. That there is a close relationship to the Bible is not surprising since the first Hebrew patriarch, Abraham, had come from a people related to the Assyrians in Mesopotamia. The Assyrian creation epic, *Enuma Elish,* speaks of an initial watery chaos and uses seven tablets that correspond to the biblical seven days of creation. The separation of the heaven from the earth is also there and the order of events is the same. A Nippurian myth describes a paradise where the rib is recognized as the source of life, and the eating of certain plants results in a curse. The Gilgamesh Epic describes a great flood. All of these confirm and reflect the Mesopotamian origins of the Hebrews, who presumably brought their legends and myths with them, but later modified them to reflect their new monotheism.

The two Genesis stories are remarkably different in content and tone. We will explore the first in this chapter and the second in the next two chapters because each has something different to bring to us.

The First Creation Story

The first story, in which God completed his creation in seven days, is written in somewhat poetic form and is notably devoid of anything supernatural, except that God was the power and the inspiration behind the creation. In comparison with other creation epics of the time that tell of the earth created from the body of a divided god or resting on the back of a turtle, this presentation is extremely sophisticated. It appears as a straightforward chronology of creation events. A close examination will reveal that this is a description of the natural world based on the understanding of 3,000 years ago. There are no forbidden fruits and no talking snakes. There are simple observations of the world as early people saw it, and from these observations they made logical conclusions about creation. This was an ancient form of science.

> In the beginning when God created the heavens and the
> earth, the earth was a formless void and darkness covered
> the face of the deep, while a wind from [*or the Spirit of*] God
> swept over the face of the waters. Then God said, "Let there
> be light"; and there was light. God saw that the light was
> good; and God separated the light from the darkness. God
> called the light Day, and the darkness he called Night. And
> there was evening and there was morning, the first day.
> (Genesis 1:1-5)(NRSV)

The primeval earth was presumed formless and void—an empty slate for the Creator to fill. It was certainly inspiration that gave the writer the idea of a chaotic initial state for the earth, because there could be no real evidence for it, except perhaps in the violence of an earthquake. As we shall see, this formlessness is close to the way science today envisions the newly formed planet. After the sky and the earth, the next thing created was light, and a separation was made of the light from the darkness. The first day was born. The creation of light before the creation of the sun on the fourth day may seem illogical to us and an observational error, but to these early observers, light and day were not dependent on the sun. After all, light appears before the sun rises and remains for some time after the last edge of the sun slips below the horizon. This is a statement of observational fact that was perfectly logical to primitive man who was unaware that the atmosphere diffuses the light of the sun and gives us a gradual dawn and dusk. On planets with no atmosphere, sunrise and sunset are sharply defined.

> And God said, "Let there be a dome in the midst of the
> waters, and let it separate the waters from waters." So
> God made the dome and separated the waters that were
> under the dome from the waters that were above the
> dome. And it was so. God called the dome Sky. And
> there was evening and there was morning, the second
> day. (Genesis 1:6-8)(NRSV)

Indeed, the sky does appear to be a dome above a flat earth, and this was a concept held by most ancient peoples. The sun and the moon and the stars all passed on the under surface of this dome. We, who know otherwise, don't think in this way, but just look at a clear blue sky and you can easily see why this was the earliest understanding of the heavens. It was wrong, but based on the visual evidence that early peoples had, the concept of the dome of the sky was very rational. Since water comes from the dome of heaven in the form of rain, part of the water must be stored above the dome. These are logical interpretations of natural phenomena as experienced by the senses of early man and would be hard for the average person to disprove today without using some modern technology. Two places for water are apparent from direct observation; and indeed the clouds are celestial water reservoirs. Early man probably did not yet know that evaporation of the water from the surface of the earth was the source of heavenly water. After all evaporation is an invisible phenomenon that must await indirect evidence. (This appears to be known by the time of Isaiah. See Isaiah 55:10.)

> And God said, "Let the waters under the sky be gathered together into one place and let the dry land appear." And it was so. God called the dry land Earth and the waters that were gathered together he called Seas. And God saw that it was good. The God said, "Let the earth put forth vegetation: plants yielding seed, and fruit trees of every kind on earth that bear fruit with the seed in it." And it was so. The earth brought forth vegetation: plants yielding seed of every kind, and trees of every kind bearing fruit with the seed in it. And God saw that it was good. And there was evening and there was morning, the third day. (Genesis 1:9-13)(NRSV)

The land was then formed by separation of the waters below the dome, as God worked on the third day. Being creatures of the land, early humans realized that almost all of our sustenance comes from the land. (Today, we sometimes lose sight of this fact.) Apparently, these early people had seen the ocean and had a sense of the vast amount of water present on the earth, for they give primacy to the water. Perhaps, the periodic flooding of the Mesopotamian plain suggested that, or the fact that there is water underground if wells were dug. But land was required for humans to live upon and so God ordered it to be formed. Then on the third day, after the dry land had appeared, it was logical for plants to be created. The order of creation as listed has always been confusing, because plants were created before the sun was created and even early peoples probably knew that plants require light for growth. Indeed, if they had tried to grow plants in the dark of their houses, they soon failed. But as we have discussed earlier, to these ancient people, light was independent of the sun; light was that which defined the day—light had been created in Day One.

Finally there is a strong emphasis upon the trees that bear fruit with seeds. Both ancient farmers and hunter-gatherers had great dependency upon use of trees bearing fruits and nuts. How dull our diet today would be without them.

> And God said, "Let there be lights in the dome of the sky to separate the day from the night; and let them be for signs and for seasons and for days and for years, and let them be lights in the dome of the sky to give light upon the earth." And it was so. God made the two great lights—the greater light to rule the day and the lesser light to rule the night— and the stars. God set them in the dome of the sky to give light upon the earth, to rule over the day and over the night, and to separate the light from the darkness. And God saw that it was good. And there was evening and there was morning, the fourth day. (Genesis 1:14-19)(NRSV)

It was then on the fourth day that the heavens are completed with the lights to rule the day and the night. These were to shine brighter light on the earth and to mark the separation of day from night. Without the sun and the moon there would be no well-defined shadows to differentiate light from darkness. The movements of the sun and the moon gave order to the lives of ancient people, and a means for measuring months and years, seasons for planting and harvest, and times for religious festivals. It was many centuries before it was generally understood that the earth was a sphere and the spinning of the earth on its axis caused the sun to appear to be rising and setting. Such information was not commonly accepted in the ancient world, for it was not immediately obvious from experience and it took indirect evidence to prove it. Yet by early in the fifth century BC, the early Greeks had determined that the earth was a sphere largely from the shape of the shadow of the earth in lunar eclipses. By the second century BC, Eratosthenes had calculated, to some degree of accuracy, the circumference of the earth. Ironically, when the church became more powerful, theology forced a reversion back to a flat earth concept based on the Bible. (Job 37:3, among others, speaks of the corners of the earth, implying a flat earth.)

> And God said, "Let the waters bring forth swarms of living creatures, and let birds fly above the earth across the dome of the sky." So God created the great sea monsters and every living creature that moves, of every kind, with which the waters swarm, and every winged bird of every kind. And God saw that it was good. God blessed them, saying, "Be fruitful and multiply and fill the waters in the seas, and let birds multiply on the earth." And there was evening and there was morning, the fifth day. (Genesis 1:20-23)(NRSV)

To fill his earth, finally on the fifth day, God created the birds, the fish, and the insects. It must have been inspiration that the ancient people sensed these creatures were more ancient than mammals and gave them an earlier entrance onto creation's stage, which is in accordance with evolution. But they didn't really have any evidence that this was so, except that they seemed to be less advanced creatures than mammals. In any case, it was apparent to these people that all animals ultimately utilized plants as food and they logically made sure that the first hungry creatures would emerge into a world full of fresh vegetation.

> And God said, "Let the earth bring forth living creatures of every kind: cattle and creeping things and wild animals of the earth of every kind." And it was so. God made the wild animals of the earth of every kind, and the cattle of every kind, and everything that creeps upon the ground of every kind. And God saw that it was good. (Genesis 1:24-25)(NRSV)

The sixth day was then reserved for mammals, a recognition, perhaps, of their current dominance over the rest of the animal kingdom, particularly in size and intelligence. It is interesting that in the creation of the plants (third day), the creation of birds, insects, and sea creatures (fifth day), and the creation of the mammals and land creatures (sixth day), God called for the waters and the earth to bring them forth. The implication, based on the time scale of six days, is of course that God created them instantly, but actually he is calling them forth out of the substance in which each live, to be created out of that environment, to be shaped by its requirements. Today from science, we know that to be the case. It was perhaps obvious to the early authors of this beautiful creation story, but it was also inspired thinking.

> Then God said, "Let us make humankind in our image, according to our likeness; and let them have dominion over the fish of the sea, and over the birds of the air, and over the cattle, and over all the wild animals of the earth, and over every creeping thing that creeps upon the earth."
> So God created humankind in his image
> In the image of God he created them.
> Male and female he created them.
> God blessed them, and God said to them, "Be fruitful and multiply, and fill the earth and subdue it; and have dominion over the fish of the sea and over the birds of the

air and over every living thing that moves upon the earth."
God said, "See, I have given you every plant yielding seed
that is upon the face of the earth, and every tree with tree
with seed in its fruit; you shall have them for food. And to
every beast of the earth, and to every bird of the air, and to
everything that creeps on the earth, everything that has the
breath of life, I have given every green plant for food." And
it was so. God saw everything that he had made, and indeed,
it was very good. And there was evening and there was
morning, the sixth day. (Genesis 1:26-31)(NRSV)

It is probably due to an awareness of the closeness of humans
to the other mammals, that on the sixth day, after the animals
appeared, we also have the creation of humans, male and female.
The Hebrew word used here for humans is *adam* and it has
traditionally been translated as man, but this New Revised Standard
version of the Bible has correctly translated it as humankind for
that is undoubtedly the sense intended. Here we have no male
priority, but instead men and women are created equally as human
beings. Here there is no cloak of mythological inferiority cast upon
women to be worn undeserved for ages. They are created as full
partners in the business of being fruitful, multiplying and filling
the earth, but also in subduing it. Humans are created as the
ultimate goal of God's creation, intelligent creatures that were able
to take over the stewardship of his creation. Human beings were
understood to have powers of thought far beyond their mammalian
relatives—they had a godlike "image." It is probable that the author
of this story even believed human physical appearance was actually
like God's. I suppose, God could present himself anthropologically
if he chose, but the ancient writer was most aware of the creative
and logical nature of the human intelligence, which gave
extraordinary power, almost supernatural in comparison with
that of their animal cousins. It is sometimes suggested that
human superiority is vanity, but even the simplest man of old
was aware of the vast difference in brain power between man
and animals.

> Thus the heavens and the earth were finished, and all their multitude. And on the seventh day God finished the work that he had done, and he rested on the seventh day from all the work he had done. So God blessed the seventh day and hallowed it, because on it God rested from all the work that he had done in creation. (Genesis 2:1-3)(NRSV)

On the seventh day, God rested. The work was completed. He was tired from his labor. The tendency to anthropomorphize (humanize) God was common in that age, and we must all admit that we still do it today. Does a spirit God tire? We cannot know, but any being that has to relate to humans over eons is bound to get tired. So here God, through the Hebrews, also gave humanity a day of rest. Not only did this allow people to rest from their labors at least one day out of seven; it also gave them a sacred, holy day that was a day for their God. It was revolutionary and so inspired that practically the entire world had adopted it at one time. Today, in the pressures of modern living, we are beginning to lose it, and we lose it to our peril. We need a day of rest and a day for God.

The seven-day creation timetable is thought to be the major source of our concept of the seven-day week. Other ancient peoples observed different groupings of days; the Greeks had no week at all and the Romans originally had an eight-day week with the eighth day reserved for the market and a school holiday. By the third century AD, the Jewish and Christian influence had changed the Roman week to seven days. Possibly, the seven-day week evolved from the four phases of the roughly twenty-eight-day lunar cycle: full, waning, new, and waxing. The number seven may represent the seven heavenly bodies known to the ancients, the sun, the moon, and the five observable planets: Mercury, Venus, Mars, Jupiter, and Saturn. Other than that, there are no other astronomical systems that would generate a seven-day period. The seven-day week, therefore, must rank as one of the more important cultural concepts the world has inherited from the early Hebrews.

What is demonstrated by this first account is that early people were eagerly observing their world and trying to make some sense out of it. They did not hesitate to hypothesize about relationships of things and their origins. They were, in a sense, scientists working with the understanding that they had. What they didn't conceive of was the vast length of time that the creation took. Humans, with their short life-spans, could only imagine humanly possible times.

This timetable is, unfortunately, the center of the problem that occurs with creationists in regard to the first creation story. In the seventeenth century, by calculating from biblical dates, Bishop Ussher determined that God began creation at 2:30 in the afternoon on Sunday, October 23, 4004, BC. And someone asked, "And pray, Holy Father, what was God doing before he created the universe?" Ussher angrily retorted, "Creating hell for those who ask questions such as that!" Of course, that date is totally ridiculous. Egyptian civilization goes back a thousand years before that. A more recent evaluation of the biblical data has established a date of approximately 10,000 years ago which is widely accepted by creationists. This is still completely refuted by geological evidence which establishes the age of the earth at some 5 billion years and the light from many galaxies that can be seen by the Hubble telescope has taken many times longer than that to reach us. The creationists forget Peter's figurative warning that time looks different to an infinite God.

> But do not ignore this one fact, beloved, that with the Lord
> one day is like a thousand years, and a thousand years are
> like one day. (2 Peter 3: 8)(NRSV)

One important feature of this first creation story is that God was continually reviewing his handiwork and declaring it to be good. His only conversation with humans was in blessing. This account is positive and encouraging for here humans are created in God's image, intellectually and spiritually. There is no doubt the early author considered himself blessed.

The Second Creation Story

> In the day that the Lord God made the earth and the heavens,
> when no plant of the field was yet in the earth and no herb
> of the field had yet sprung up—for the Lord God had not
> caused it to rain upon the earth, and there was no one to till
> the ground; but a stream would rise from the earth, and
> water the whole face of the ground—then the Lord God
> formed man from the dust of the ground, and breathed
> into his nostrils the breath of life; and the man became a
> living being. (Genesis 2:4*b*-7)(NRSV)

The second Genesis creation story (Genesis 2:4*b*-4:26) is dramatically different from the first, and we should point out some of the differences here. Instead of listing the creation from the formation of the earth, it begins with the creation of *adam* meaning mankind. Here mankind is represented by a single man who is not named by God, but who assumes the name Adam. In some versions of the Bible, this does not occur until Genesis 4:25, but in others that name is ascribed to him as early as 2:20*b*. Here humans are the first creature of creation rather than the last; even plants have not yet "sprung up." But the most notable feature of the second story is that here we find more mythological elements.

Note:

> Adam is created from the "dust" of the earth,
> After which God "breathes" life into him,
> A garden is planted for him to live in,
> A tree is there whose forbidden fruit gives knowledge of
>   good and evil,
> A tree of life is there that could grant divinity,
> All creatures are created as possible companions for Adam,
> Adam's rib is the source of Eve,
> And there is a snake that talks.

Undoubtedly, much of this story, which has parallels in the Sumerian mythology, was designed to explain why humanity did not feel particularly blessed by its lot in life. Although this storyteller used some mythological elements to tell us some great truths, his story is extremely important because he is not as concerned about creation as about relationships—the relationships between humanity and the Creator God and between humans and their fellow human beings. And since these relationships are tragically broken, this storyteller felt humanity was cursed, not blessed, and he managed to blame women for the troubles. He also blamed the source of sin on the poor snake, a sometimes poisonous creature, not too well liked anyway for all his slithering around. (Note that the serpent was not meant to represent the devil, as some have claimed, because the concept of Satan had not appeared among the Hebrews at this early date. See chapter 3.)

This negative review should not imply that there are no important theological and scientific concepts found in the second story. The reality of sin and evil in the world is not to be ignored or passed over lightly. We shall return to this account again in the next two chapters and see that the details of this familiar story represent some extremely important concepts concerning the reality of creation that are not addressed in the first story.

The Creation Story of Science

Let us now look at what science has to say about creation. Is it really as anti-Christian as some would have us believe? Rather, there is much in the evidence that scientists have uncovered about creation that speaks to us as Christians. Before we continue, it should be re-emphasized that what one believes about creation and the stories in the first several chapters of Genesis in no way determines whether or not you are a "true" Christian. If instructions to the contrary are found in the Bible, I have not seen them.

The cornerstone of modern understanding of creation is the "big bang." Although, there is some rejection of this, most modern cosmologists currently feel the big bang is what started it all, and considerable evidence has been accumulated in its support. What this means is that the entire universe and time itself can be conceived of as coming from a single originating event. But it is at this frontier of knowledge that science has come to an impasse. There is no cause for the big bang, only God. There is no reason for the big bang, only God. What most scientists think is that the universe had a beginning. No longer do they believe that it always was and always will be. Like everything that we know on earth, the universe had a beginning—a birth—and presumably will also have an end—a death.

The big bang theory was developed from an astronomical discovery made as recently as 1924 by Edwin Hubble. He found those "fuzzy stars" seen through telescopes were actually other galaxies made up of billions of stars just like our own Milky Way galaxy. The interesting property that he found common to all the galaxies was that they were speeding away from us and from each other. In fact, Einstein's equations had originally predicted just that, but he changed them because he failed to believe them. This meant that the universe was expanding like a balloon, as if exploding. And if the universe was expanding, then at one point it must have been much closer together, even all together at a single point, a single instant of time—the moment of creation, the big bang. From the velocity of the expansion, it has been calculated that this occurred about 13.7 billion years ago. From that instant all that we know today has developed, including time itself. One of the strongest confirmations of this theory came when scientists were able to measure the faint background radiation left over from the big bang. It appears as faint radio hiss and can be seen as some of the snow on your TV screen when it is not tuned to a channel. A large amount of other data supports the big bang concept. Perhaps, something will be discovered in the future that refutes this theory, but for now it reigns supreme in the science-of-the-beginning.

At the moment of the big bang, all of the natural laws had already been created; all the forces and dimensions had been conceived. All the laws of chance were in place to be used by a loving God to carefully direct his creation. It may be, as has been suggested, that what we see as natural laws, preexistent in the universe before creation, are just extensions of laws controlling the spiritual universe. These laws were necessary to shape the nature of the physical universe that was created in the big bang.

In an instant, matter and energy were formed from nothing— from empty space. Physicist John A. Wheeler is reported to have said, "That empty space is not empty. It is the seat of the most violent physics." Although it appears illogical, scientists theorize that the entire universe came into being from empty space. As we will discuss later in chapter 9, matter at this level has strange properties. Actually, the temperature in that earliest time was so high that atoms and molecules, as we understand them, did not exist. Instead, only fundamental subnuclear particles such as quarks and gluons were present. These strange things, among the most basic forms of matter, are really types of matter-energy thought to exist in a multidimensional space where they behave in unusual ways, totally unlike large-scale matter that we know. Yet it is of these strange things that all atoms and molecules and thus we ourselves are made.

Within three minutes, the universe had cooled to the point where the first atoms of the simplest of all the elements, hydrogen, could form. Three-fourths of the universe today is hydrogen that was created in the big bang. The hydrogen atoms in you and in the water you drink were made at the beginning of creation. Most of the rest of the universe is helium. The other elements account for only a trace of the matter in the universe.

The hydrogen became concentrated by gravity into enormous clouds to form gargantuan proto-galaxies, and after several billion years the hydrogen in the proto-galaxies condensed into huge stars. Having relatively short lifetimes, these giant stars soon spent their hydrogen fuel, and as they died, their nuclear fires produced all of the other larger elements. In their final moments, the stars exploded, spewing the elements into space. It is now thought that the residues collapsed into what astronomers call "black holes." A "black hole," is the tiny remnant of a star where mass and gravity is so concentrated that even light cannot escape from it. The strong gravity attracted other stars and thus galaxies such as our own Milky Way were born. In the fiery arms of these galaxies, new stars were created even as they are being created today. We can truly say that everything we touch and see around us, including the atoms in our own bodies, was created in a star. We are not only made of the "dust of the earth"—we are made of star dust.

In one of the spiral arms of the Milky Way, an enormous cloud of star dust was bombarded by waves of gravity from nearby exploding stars called supernova, and the star dust began to coalesce again into a giant rotating disk of matter. When the hydrogen in the central core of the disk became dense enough, the force of gravity re-ignited the nuclear furnaces and a medium-sized star, the sun, began to shine. Its light illuminated the other smaller aggregates of matter that were orbiting the infant star. As their gravity increased, these aggregates gradually collected the material around them, and thus the planets were formed about 5 billion years ago. The sun in its earliest stages raged fiercely and burned off all of the lighter matter, including water, from the four innermost planets, which we now call Mercury, Venus, Earth, and Mars. The outer planets escaped this purging fire by being too far away, and they remained as huge gaseous spheres. But the purging by fire was necessary because it gave the earth solid ground for a future intelligent creature to walk upon.

Some astronomers believe that after it had cooled sufficiently from the sun's scorching heat, the barren earth was replenished with water from icy comets which pelted the cooling infant planet. Others feel the water came from out-gassing of the water trapped in rocks deeper in the earth, through earthquakes and volcanoes. Probably, both sources were responsible for the vast amount of water we now have. Of course, to us, it is a lot of water, but astronomically, the water only forms a thin film over two-thirds of the planet. However it came, the water filled the lowlands and formed primeval lakes, seas, and oceans. All this water could only survive on a planet both warm enough and cool enough to maintain water in the liquid form. Mercury is too hot because it is too close to the sun. Venus may have had water, but today it is too hot (700°C) because it is covered by a thick heat-trapping cloud cover.

Mars, which *Voyager* spacecraft pictures suggest had liquid water in its ancient past, is now arid and cold. Indeed, there is only a narrow band of space in which liquid water occurs. Everywhere else is too hot or too cold. Only Earth survived as a wet, beautiful sphere of blue and white—the perfect home for life.

And then, about 4 billion years ago in the warm water of those melted-comet oceans, something happened. The first life appeared. Many scientists believe this happened by chance in a soup of carbon-containing molecules swirling in some tidal pool on a prehistoric shore. Comets may have brought with them enormous amounts of these molecules. It has been recently estimated that Haley's comet alone contains carbon compounds equivalent to 10 percent of the earth's biomass.

Perhaps, it was lightning or ultraviolet radiation that started the process. But experiments to reproduce this have only formed tars and residues containing some of the chemicals of life; they did not produce living matter from the unliving. As Christians who believe that God can intervene in the physical world, we feel God was uniquely involved in the creation of life, for God is the original living being, and life, to date, only comes from previous life. In 1892, when science had only recently realized that life did not still spontaneously generate on earth, Henry Drummond wrote in his book *Natural Laws in the Spiritual World,*

> No change of substance, no modification of environment, no chemistry, no electricity, nor any form of energy, nor any evolution can endow any single atom of the mineral world with the attribute of life. It is as if God had placed everything in earth and heaven in the hands of Nature, but reserved a point at the genesis of Life for His direct appearing.

Modern science has yet to prove him wrong.

No matter how primitive this early life was, it consisted of an arrangement of matter that became something more than a mixture of chemicals. There was no breaking of the second law of thermodynamics which indicates that disorder should prevail, for that only applies to closed systems like the universe as a whole. Open systems, such as the living cell, are driven by energy that can come in and go out, and these can exist in spite of the second law. As we shall see, life happened within God's universal laws, for life is not exempt from the natural laws but depends on them for its existence. In fact, it is because of these laws that life has been able to become so complex. Perhaps, the creation of life will some day be duplicated in the laboratory, but that in no way proves that God was not involved—it will only prove that a preexistent intelligent life was necessary for it to happen.

Most scientists and astronomers today believe that the universe formed by just such an outline. Does this really conflict with the biblical view of creation? In detail, perhaps. But it corroborates the biblical concept of a beginning—a genesis. It describes a universe of matter and energy created from nothing as if from the thought of God. It allows for the creation of life, even intelligent life, from inanimate matter, "the dust of the earth," a process we may never understand but which we know has occurred at least once.

To some scientists who cannot believe a supernatural source for anything, life is just an accident and intelligent life even more so. But there is no rationale for intelligence to occur in a universe without a designer—in a universe created entirely by accident. For what purpose would that have happened? Why would quarks and gluons, those tiny bits of multidimensional energy, have the amazing property to form intelligent life and awareness of themselves, if they did not fulfill a creator's purpose? Why would the universe have so many interrelated forces and complex energies, so many billions of galaxies, so many trillions of stars without someone to be aware of them? Without a creator's purpose, why should living things be formed at all? Why should a universe be formed at all? It seems difficult to comprehend such a meaningless existence. The very fact that we exist at all is the best proof we have that life has a purpose. As people of that purpose, we can see that our modern scientific understanding of creation only makes it more clear that "in the beginning God created the heavens and the earth" (Genesis 1:1).

CHAPTER TWO

EVOLUTION IS NOT A
FOUR-LETTER WORD

When I look at your heavens,
the work of your fingers,
the moon and stars that you have established;
what are human beings that you
are mindful of them,
mortals that you care for them?
Yet you have made them a little lower than God,
and crowned them with glory and honor.
You have given them dominion
over the works of your hands;
you have put all things under their feet, . . .
(Psalm 8:3-6)(NRSV)

For some Christians, to even mention the word "evolution" is committing the greatest of heresies. One day, one of my Sunday school class members, a dear elderly lady, declared that all the evil in the world is because of the "evolutionists." To such people this is the ultimate evil, an atheistic concept from the devil being forced upon the world, and the basis for all lack of belief in the Bible and God.

This is also somewhat ironic because the Bible itself displays a clear "evolution" in the understanding of God. Originally Abraham thought he was the chief Canaanite god El. Then he became the tribal God of the Hebrews who was located first on top of Mount

Sinai and then in a pillar of fire in the wilderness. The Hebrews were somewhat ambivalent about him. He was responsible for evil as well as good, and could sometimes be a violent, unforgiving war God. But he was also a loving God who put up with a lot from his unfaithful people. When the temple was destroyed, he was understood to be everywhere, but still, almost exclusively the God of the Jews. Finally, with Jesus he is revealed as a loving father of the whole world.

So "evolution" is not a concept foreign to the Bible. Yet many Christians have been told that evolution in creation is wrong. As a result, there is a significant portion of the Christian world actively in disbelief of an important fact about God's creation. These people fail to understand that evolution is the way God worked and continues to work in creating the world. Such ignorance is tragic for we can learn much about ourselves and about God from the revelation that comes to us through evolution.

Evolution is the method God uses for the development of life-forms on this planet, and it is so strongly supported by scientific evidence that it is no longer just a theory but a fact, and literally a fact-of-life. Your acceptance or not of evolution should be based on the overwhelming scientific evidence, not on whether you believe in the Bible or not. Evolution is the description of the way in which God chose to create us. It is as real as the earth itself, and we as Christians must come to terms with that fact. For if God created the world and all that lives on it, then he must have created all living things through evolution. It is presumptuous and somewhat irreverent to refuse to accept God's method, a method that he has revealed to us through science, and instead, insist that some ancient sage knew how it was done. Notice how God admonished Job for questioning his methods.

> Who are you to question my wisdom with your ignorant, empty words? Stand up now like a man and answer the questions I ask you. Were you there when I made the world? If you know so much, tell me about it. (Job 38: 2-4)(TEV)

By using modern methods to study the fossil record, scientists, called paleontologists, can put together the outline of how life formed and changed. Although their understanding is still incomplete, God has given us, through modern science, the privilege denied Job—a glimpse of our beginnings—creation as he really created it.

Evolution is about God's creation of life on the physical world and therefore, it is a physical world phenomenon which can be studied by scientists. Although we cannot live in earlier epochs to witness the creatures of the past, God has given us a means to observe them through their fossils. Fossils are the forms and skeletons of living organisms that have been mineralized and thus preserved in the rocks. By studying their remains in various rock strata laid down over millions of years, an evolution of life can be observed.

The evidence for evolution is enormous. An entire panoply of fossilized life-forms are visible in the rocks, with all of the simpler organisms occurring in the most ancient rock strata, and the more complex species in the younger layers. The change of one life-form into other forms is readily traced in the fossil record. Where gaps occur, it is usually because the fossils have not yet been found, or the creature's skeleton was never fossilized. Both fossil formation and discovery are very much chance events. For a fossil to form, the creature had to die in a place or condition that would allow the bones to be submerged in mud or volcanic ash and then be converted to rock over the ages. Then this rock had to lifted by geological forces and eroded so that it was accessible for fossil hunters today. Neither event was a common occurrence. Although *Tyrannosaurus rex* may be the most famous dinosaur, only a few complete fossilized skeletons have been found to date.

Another reason for apparent gaps in the evolutionary ladder is because evolutionary changes may have taken place in a portion of a species that had become geographically isolated. Due to a different environment in the new location, this branch of the species became, over time, so different from the original that they could no longer interbreed—a new species was formed. When the land was altered by geological upheavals or climatic changes, it was sometimes possible for the new species to re-enter the region of the original animals. The new species, having become superior in some way, eventually dominated the old form which had remained unchanged in its stable environment. The geological fossil record would then show a dramatic change in the species in the original region with no intermediate forms present in the gap, because those forms had evolved somewhere else.

Apparent gaps can also occur when the environment is stable and creatures are successfully living in it. Their species can remain relatively unchanged for millions of years. But when its environment is changing, the species will change more rapidly too. Therefore, there may be only small populations of intermediate species that are much less likely to become fossilized, and large populations of the stable forms that have a greater chance to be fossilized. All of this can lead to gaps in the fossil record resulting in what has been labeled as the artifact called "punctuated evolution."

It doesn't always require fossils to witness evolution. Evolutionary changes can be witnessed in geographically isolated species living today in places like the Galapagos Islands and Hawaii. The Galapagos are located in the Pacific Ocean six hundred miles off the coast of South America. It was here that naturalist Charles Darwin visited on his epic voyage on the ship, the *Beagle*. From the specimens he obtained and carried home, he was able to develop the revolutionary concept of evolution. And the Galapagos still remain one of the most exciting places for biologists to witness the changes that can be made in living things. When the islands emerged from the ocean as the tops of active underwater volcanoes, they were barren black volcanic rocks. Eventually both plants and animals found their way there and over time they began to change. The most significant change in most of the animals was in their color. They all became darker, to better blend in with the dark volcanic rock and soil. A few finches arrived after the plants had been established, and from this one original finch species, there are now fully thirteen species of finches that can be found nowhere else. All of them are closely related, but they differ significantly in their beaks. Each one of the thirteen different kinds of finches feeds on a different type or part of the plants. They range from long curving beaks to get to the base of a tubular flower or fruit, to short stubby beaks to crack hard seeds. Even the fish and aquatic animals, many totally unique, are modifications of the original species that arrived before the rise of the land bridge of Panama, which closed off the Pacific from the Caribbean. And the Galapagos was named for its tortoises. These huge lumbering reptiles are the dominant land animals, filling the large herbivore niche that the antelope fills in Africa.

One aspect of evolution that we often fail to realize is the enormous amount of time that evolution has been going on. With our short life span we usually can't see its slow, steady pace. We observe only a few decades of life, an insignificant period in the history of life on the earth. Only a few changing species have been observed in the period of human history, such as the changes that have occurred in some of the animals brought to Hawaii with the first Polynesian settlers. The darkening of the color of moths living on soot-stained trees in industrial England has been observed. But in general, most significant changes take thousands of generations.

We do see evolution occurring in bacteria that quickly have evolved resistance to our antibiotics. With very short generation times and life spans, bacteria can undergo thousands of generations very rapidly. When we become ill and take an antibiotic, most of the bacteria are killed. But if only a few of the most resistant bacteria remain, they will reproduce and eventually the population of bacteria will be resistant to the antibiotic. This rapid evolution due to very short generation times has become a major problem in health care today. There are strains of staphylococci and TB that have evolved resistance to all available antibiotics and are, therefore, very dangerous.

Another important point about evolution is that it appears to be a necessary aspect of life. Living organisms, *by their very design*, will evolve to fit their environment, and to thus maximize their chance of survival. Environment determines the form life will take, because of what biologists call "survival of the fittest." It is built into the mechanisms of life. Only those individuals that can successfully grow to maturity will be able to reproduce and thus ensure survival of their kind. An interesting example of this took place in modern times in Japan where fishermen were harvesting a variety of crab that had a randomly curved and cratered shell. Occasionally, a crab would appear that bore a resemblance to the face of a samurai warrior. The superstitious fishermen, believing that such crabs contained the spirit of the dead samurai, were loath to eat them and threw them back into the sea. With this form of "natural" selection, today most of those crabs look like samurai warriors, because they were the fittest and survived most often to breed their own kind. Just look at the other results human selection has bred into the plants and animals that serve us. Today it is hard to realize that a dachshund has been evolved from its ancestral wolf.

Different environments will give different forms to the life that can live there. Dolphins and whales, for instance, mammals which went back to live in the sea, look more like fish than they look like hippos, their relatives who live on the land. Bats have wings like birds who also share the airways, and ostriches, who don't fly, have long legs and run like antelope across the land. It is just the way life is. The design is very elegant for a geologically active planet that is subject to continents that shift, volcanoes that explode, earthquakes that uplift the earth, floods and droughts, glaciers and winds that all shape and reshape the world. God was not required to constantly re-invent creatures for each change in the environment; his original design had the built-in mechanism to make all the changes as needed. A creation that kept on creating was exactly what the designer needed.

And diversity in life-forms is also built into evolution. The millions of plant and animal species that are present on the earth today and the billions of forms that were present eons ago, but are now extinct, all illustrate the beauty and infinite variety that an evolutionary creation provides. Every ecological niche is filled. Every opportunity to make a living is taken advantage of. And the beautiful wonder of it all is that God designed life to do that. And the elegant design is based on a long coded molecule called deoxyribonucleic acid (DNA). This combination of the atoms of carbon, hydrogen, oxygen, nitrogen, and phosphorus is what determines the form of all of life. Because it can be mutated by simple changes in parts of the molecule which change the code, the form of life can change. And change it has—until we have the marvelous array of plants and animals that we see around us—and we have us. No one can deny that we—the most intelligent and yet most destructive creature ever to live on earth—are the top animal of the evolutionary ladder.

And some scientists think that our evolution can be detected in our own genes. From our genes are generated all the proteins needed to control our bodies and give it structure and function.

These genes, made up of DNA, contain all the information needed to produce every cell in our bodies and tell each cell what to do and when to do it. Yet to make us requires only 1 percent of all the information stored in our genes. Why would God give us all that extra baggage if he had created us just as we are today? It has been suggested that the other 99 percent of the genes tell the story of the creatures from which we have evolved, since no gene is ever lost; it is just shut off and not used. In the evolution of life-forms, these earlier genes can be reactivated and reappear in a later creature where they may be useful in the species' struggle to survive its changing environment. When all of our genes can be read, perhaps we will see the full story of our evolution from the first form of life to ourselves. Each cell in our bodies, therefore, may contain the entire record of our evolution.

The Evolving Story

Since evolution is apparently the way that God created us, let us continue the story of creation that we started in the last chapter and observe the evolutionary unfolding of God's beautiful plan.

God created life when the earth was ready to accept it and nourish it. From the inanimate chemical broth of some tidal pool on the edge of the sea, he fashioned a chemical mixture, possibly enclosed in a film of oil. It was the correct combination of molecules that gave it the special properties of growth and reproduction that became the first living thing. Very primitive in form and chemistry initially, the first organism no longer exists. Life has changed so much and become so complex that we cannot even conceive of what it could be without the complex design we know today. The first firmly documented evidence of life on this planet is that of a bacterium-like organism that evolved some 3.5-3.8 billion years ago. That is not very long after the earth was formed from stellar debris about 5 billion years ago.

Modern bacteria, tiny bags of chemicals dissolved and suspended in water and bound to fatty membranes, are still extremely complex. Although one of the simplest forms of life, they utilize the same genetic codes and fundamental chemistries found in all life today, indicating that these processes were present very early. Although most of the molecules of life that we have now are enormously improved over the originals, these original molecules were sophisticated enough to change the world forever.

We are all descendants in an unbroken chain from the original organism, as through the ages new life-forms evolved. But things moved slowly. By 3 billion years ago, some of the bacteria had developed the ability to harness the energy of sunlight and had begun to make use of the enormous quantities of carbon dioxide present in the atmosphere. These tiny organisms called blue-green algae had a profound effect on the atmosphere. With the energy of sunlight, they were able to split water molecules into hydrogen and oxygen, using the hydrogen atoms to convert carbon dioxide to carbohydrates and releasing the unneeded, poisonous oxygen into the atmosphere. This process called photosynthesis goes on today in every plant, and it determined, forever after, the kind of life that would live on earth. Previously the organisms that had evolved were fit for the primitive atmosphere that contained little if any oxygen. Oxygen was as deadly to them as too much carbon dioxide is to us. There are still many such "anaerobic" or air-poisoned bacteria living today in oxygen-poor environments, such as mud and rotting vegetation.

Now, new types of life appeared—larger and more active forms. Life that not only could tolerate the toxic gas, oxygen, but could use it to generate energy by "burning or oxidizing" the carbohydrates back to carbon dioxide and water. Like burning gas in your furnace or gasoline in your car, this oxidation created large amounts of biological energy that eventually put animals on the move. But it was the same energy that had originally come from the sun, just transformed and put to use by life. Indeed, when the Genesis scientist wrote that God said, "I have provided all kinds of grain and all kinds of fruit for you to eat; but for all the wild animals and for all the birds I have provided grass and leafy plants for food" (Genesis 1:29-30), he was recognizing that plants actually supply all of the energy that animals use. We now know that all of that energy ultimately comes from the sun.

Still bacteria were the only life-forms on earth for billions of years, reaching a wide diversity in form about 2 billion years ago. For more than half of the time that life has been on the earth, bacteria were the only life-forms present. In sheer numbers they are probably still the dominant form. But then something special happened that had another profound effect: The first cells containing a nucleus appeared. Called "eukaryotic" or "good kernel" cells, their nucleus encapsulated the reproductive DNA molecules. The DNA comprised the genes that direct all activities of the cell, the formation, the life, and even the death of the cells. These genes are present in larger structures called the chromosomes. In bacteria, this genetic material is distributed throughout the cell, but in eukaryotic cells this material is confined to the nucleus. One theory suggests that the nucleus developed from the "symbiotic" or mutually beneficial combination of two bacteria, the one giving up all other functions to keep the genes and the ultimate control, while the other organism gave up its genes to keep all the other mechanism of life. The significance of this event is that more complex forms of life were now possible, and indeed, every plant and animal, except the bacteria and the blue-green algae, evolved from these eukaryotes which appeared 1.4 billion years ago. From this point on tremendous change occurred and an enormous variety of life-forms was able to evolve.

The changes were slow at first as the forces of natural selection and mutation began their inexorable development into more and more complex forms. The eukaryotic cells could form large clumps of cells to their mutual benefit, and eventually, some of these cells took on specialized functions for the group, such as digestion or propulsion or food gathering. By 700 million years ago, the earliest jellyfish, sponges, and sea worms were present. In another 100 million years, sea life flourished, including many strange animals such as the now-extinct trilobite, the ancestor of the horseshoe crab. And in another 200 million years (about 400 million years ago), all of the major forms of these "invertebrates" (no backbone) animals were present, and some land plants had already sent roots into the barren soil of the land. During this time, the first "vertebrates" (animals with backbones), the jawed fish, appeared, paving the way to the great vertebrate species of today. In another 50 million years, the first amphibians made that epic transition from the sea to the land, clumsily crawling out of a tidal pool. Later these creatures would evolve into the reptiles. Soon the insects also emerged from the ocean, flitting, crawling, and buzzing in the already vast swamps and jungles of the ancient landscapes. This movement onto land from the sea set the scene for the development of some of the most successful and magnificent animals to possess the earth—the dinosaurs.

For about 130 million years, from 190 to 65 million years ago, these creatures which had evolved from reptiles were the unquestioned rulers of the planet. They dominated every large-animal niche and were the all-time champions in size for any land animal ever. The enormously long-necked *Brachiosaurus* reached thirty-five tons compared to a modern elephant's five tons. Some paleontologists now believe that some of the plant-eating dinosaurs (herbivores) lived in large herds, caring for their newly hatched young. The great carnivores, such as the famous *Tyrannosaurus rex,* preyed on the herbivores, just as modern lions feed on the African wildebeest.

And hidden in the weeds and ferns, tiny, furry shrew-like creatures evolved at this time. These first mammals could do nothing but scurry about at night while the giant dinosaurs slept, biding their time until their descendants could take their place in the sun. Some scientists believe the dinosaurs were not sluggish cold-blooded reptiles, but vigorous warm-blooded competitors that completely dominated the mammals for their 130-million-year reign. Our tiny furry ancestors didn't have a chance to evolve much as long as the dinosaurs ruled.

Suddenly, by geological standards, the dinosaurs were gone. The giant creatures, who had ruled unchallenged for millions of years, were destroyed dramatically 65 million years ago. In fact, it is recognized that two other massive, but incomplete, extinctions had occurred during the reign of the dinosaurs. Scientists are certain they weren't forced into extinction by more efficient mammals, because only fossils of tiny mammals are found during the time of the dinosaurs. Instead, the mighty dinosaurs probably died out due to environmental changes. Possibly, it was a change in the climate caused by geological upheavals such as volcanoes or earthquakes, which caused sudden atmospheric cooling to which the behemoths could not adjust. Or was it due to an astronomical catastrophe?

Based on some geological evidence, today it is widely believed that a giant asteroid or comet crashed into the earth near the present-day Yucatan peninsula, sending shock and fire waves as far north as central United States. In the collision, huge clouds of dust and dirt, mixed with smoke from the ignited forests were thrown into the atmosphere. This primeval pollution could have been sufficient to blot out the sun for several years, destroying much of the plant life and depriving the dinosaurs of their primary source of food. Essentially, they starved to death.

The nature of the dinosaur demise is still hotly debated. But many scientists believe that collisions have occurred often in the history of life on the planet and these may account for the several extinctions of dinosaurs and the several extinctions of major ancient mammalian species. However it happened, the once-invincible giants vanished, leaving only their bones to tell their story.

It was during the reign of the dinosaurs that the first primitive birds appeared, still with teeth and wing claws. Their skeletal structure, their gizzards, their eggs, and their scale-derived feathers revealed a kinship to the types of dinosaurs that raced across the land on their rear legs. Although some paleontologists think they evolved directly from reptiles, many believe that several direct ancestors of the birds have been found among the dinosaurs. The two-hundred-pound predator *Deinonychus* is believed to be one of the first. Recent discoveries of feathered dinosaurs have been made in China. The feathers presumably were evolved for improved insulation and later they proved to be excellent for flying. This process scholars call "exaption," or putting structures that had evolved for another reason to a new use. Then *Archaeopteryx* appeared as the first definite birdlike creature, although it still had teeth.

Truly modern birds without teeth first appeared at the end of the Cretaceous period, just before the demise of the dinosaurs. So dinosaurs may not be gone completely. It has been suggested the bright red dinosaur that hops onto your bird feeder and the steaming roasted dinosaur that is the center of your Thanksgiving dinner may be our delightful legacies from those magnificent beasts.

Only after the dinosaurs had disappeared could the mammals emerge from their hiding places in the weeds and take their place on the evolutionary stage. Like the dinosaurs, they were able to successfully fill every large-animal niche they could find, and eventually, they lived on the land, in the seas, and in the air. Several mass extinctions occurred among the mammals too, and the last extinction, which included the giant mastodon, may have been due to a new and smarter creature that had evolved on the plains of Africa.

It was about 30 million years ago when an animal called *Aegyptopithecus* appeared, the oldest common ancestor of both apes and man. *Lucy*, the first bipedal creature in our lineage, walked the hills in Africa 3.8-2.8 million years ago. Our first tool-using ancestor, *Homo habilis* (handy man), lived about 1.8 million years ago. He was, in a sense, the first of the "humanoid" species with his larger brain size. *Homo erectus* appeared about 1.6 to 0.4 million years ago. Some believe him to be the direct ancestor of early man and the first to migrate out of Africa. His other claim to fame is that he was the first to control fire. Early man, *Homo sapiens* (wise man), appeared only 400,000 to 30,000 years ago, the first hominid truly of our species. Neanderthal man, a heavier-boned cousin of ours, lived in Europe from 130,000 to 35,000 years ago. Some experts believe that intermarriage of Neanderthals with *Homo sapiens* may have led to the typical European variety of our modern species. Recent evidence tends to show they may have been a different species that could not produce viable offspring with humans. In any case, they could not compete with their more advanced competitors and died out. The Neanderthals are known to have buried his dead with ritual objects, the oldest hominid known to do this. They are no longer considered to be a brutish dimwit for they stood fully erect and were completely modern in brain size.

Finally, maybe only 30,000 years ago (experts cannot yet agree), modern man, *Homo sapiens sapiens*, appeared—a mere novice to this game of life. Some controversial discoveries in South Africa may indicate that modern man was there as far back as 100,000 years ago, and studies of the evolution of mitochondrial DNA, which is only passed down from the mother, indicate that the female ancestor of all modern humans lived 200,000 years ago. In any case, compared with the length of time life has existed on this planet, we are almost too new to count.

A Christian Perspective

What then is a Christian to understand about all of this? Isn't it easier to believe the ancient legends and accept that God just made everything as it is right now? But that isn't the way it appears to have happened. God, in his infinite wisdom, chose to create life on earth by the process of evolution, probably because that was the best way, maybe even the only way, that it could be done. Although, it may appear that evolution is a lot of trial and error and subject to chance events with no design, we shall see in chapter 6 that such an appearance may be just the way God wanted it. God is perfectly capable of influencing the course of evolution and still remain entirely undetected, except when observed from an historical perspective and the eyes of faith.

As we have seen, one of the special features of an evolutionary creation is that all creatures are perfectly adapted to their environments, because the environment shapes their forms and abilities by the evolutionary approach to organism design. How brilliant such a mechanism seems to us humans with less brainpower than God has. As we pointed out in chapter 1, even Genesis speaks of the water and the earth bringing forth their creatures out of the environments they were to live in. Does not such a creation evoke awe and wonder in the Creator God?

In addition, because of evolution, all creatures have much the same fundamental biochemistry as we have. Mammals, being very similar to us, are therefore extremely useful as experimental models for modern medical research. The development of every wonder drug and every modern medical miracle that we know today was only possible through the sacrifice of some of our animal cousins. That could also be a reason for God to choose evolution as his route to creation.

In his book called *The Blind Watchmaker*, Richard Dawkins describes in detail how all of the variations and blind alleys of evolution are built into the nature of things and process of survival of the fittest. The fantastic diversity of life-forms develops from the very beginning in an almost mathematical manner. I am convinced that he is right. But Dawkins comes to the conclusion that there is no design to the products of evolution, incomprehensibly ignoring the design that was built into the system itself. If the discovery of a complex organism is no proof of a designer, did not the system itself that formed the organism require a designer? To use a modern example, if one found an item that had been designed and created by a computer, would that imply the computer did not require a designer? Dawkins claims it is the lazy way out to invoke the influence of an original supernatural designer since the origin of the designer is then unexplained. That, of course, assumes that there is a scientific explanation for everything—a somewhat overconfident assumption. He also feels that the intelligence of modern man is an accident or, at least, merely the result of increased complexity in the organisms as evolution progressed. Yet after 130 million years the dinosaurs did not evolve intelligence, while mammals were capable of doing it in only half that time. Was that really an accident? Surely intelligence must be the principle purpose of evolution, because without intelligence, all existence is ultimately meaningless.

What Paul Davies said about modern physics in his book, *Superforce,* could equally apply to our understanding of evolution.

> Though Science may explain the world, we still have to explain science. The laws which enable the universe to come

into being spontaneously seem themselves to be the product of exceedingly ingenious design. If physics is the product of design, the universe must have a purpose, and the evidence of modern physics suggests strongly to me that the purpose includes us.

As Christians we believe that God does things for a purpose, and we are his purpose. We also believe that he cares dearly for his creation and involves himself constantly in its care. As Jesus said,

> Are not two sparrows sold for a penny? Yet not one of them will fall to the ground apart from your Father. (Matthew 10:29)(NRSV)

From the scientific truth that life evolved over long eons of time and the Christian truth that God cares for his creation, there can be no other synthesis than that God was involved. Perhaps he allowed the original design to unfold according to the nature that he gave it. But I think that he occasionally nudged it to take another direction by orchestrating some event that to us looks like a chance occurrence. As we said, the dinosaurs were allowed 130 million years to evolve, but then were suddenly and dramatically extinguished, possibly by the cataclysmic arrival of an asteroid or comet. As I was first writing this, a fractured comet was crashing into the atmosphere of the planet Jupiter. Such occurrences do and will continue to happen. Were the dinosaurs removed because they had become incapable of evolving intelligence? Or had they served their purpose as an intermediary step, by evolving into the creatures that rule the air—the birds? Or were the dinosaurs allowed to reign until the earth had become cooler and better suited to the development of bipedal primates with large brains? Maybe in God's plan, it is only mammals that are physiologically suited to carry high levels of intelligence. We can't know for certain and can only guess that is true based on what has happened on earth. It is not human egotism that tells us we are God's plan, it is God himself.

The Second Creation Story

In our journey through evolution, we have come to the point where we must look again at the second creation story described in Genesis, the mythological one found in Genesis 2:5-3:24 depicting the Garden of Eden. Is this of no value in light of the scientific evidence of our evolutionary origins? Since all scripture is useful for teaching (2 Timothy 3:16), what can we make of it? I have already shown how it is a somewhat negative piece full of curse and failure. Does it have value yet today? From a thorough analysis of this story, it is apparent that this account is more about the beginnings of civilization than about creation of universe. Indeed, the chronology of the Bible puts Eden back at the beginnings of the earliest civilizations which occurred in the Mesopotamian valley about 5-4,000 B. C.

One interesting search for the Garden of Eden has placed it now submerged under the waters of the Persian Gulf where the ancient Tigris and Euphrates rivers once formed a fertile delta. From about 6,000-5,000 BC this region had much rainfall and abundant game. The ancient hunter-gatherers found life there to be idyllic, a paradise on earth provided by God's bountiful nature. But about this time, agriculture was invented and the nomadic hunter-gathering people came up against the farmers who began to till the fertile delta soil. Conflicts were bound to occur, much as they did in the American West when the farmers invaded the territory of the ranchers. As other regions in the area became more arid, more of the foragers arrived, but they could not compete with the advanced farmers—people called the Ubaidians. It should be noted that the Ubaidians may have established the city of Ur and Abraham may have come from these people, bringing along his ancient tribal stories of these early conflicts.

The Garden of Eden story represents the conflict between the traditional nomadic hunter-gatherers and the revolutionary settled farmers who were taking God's bounty into their own hands, relying on knowledge and their own skills rather than God. The Cain and Abel story (Genesis 4:1-16) clearly represents this competition.

Note that Cain, who is rejected by God, was a farmer, while Abel was a nomadic shepherd who had to rely on God for his pasture. The conflict is an old one.

It is not surprising that the Garden of Eden story is derived from the ancient legends of the Sumerian and related peoples of Mesopotamia. The story is rich with significance and, maybe, even based on some ancient conflicts from the very distant past. We cannot trash it as an irrelevant myth. When we look beyond the details, we see that the Eden story clearly dramatizes the human condition, a struggle between God and humans, between his creation and humans, and between human and human. We will look at it from another point of view in the next chapter.

CHAPTER THREE

YOU ANIMAL, YOU

I said in my heart with regard to human beings that God is testing them to show that they are but animals. For the fate of humans and the fate of animals is the same; as one dies, so dies the other. They all have the same breath, and humans have no advantage over the animals; for all is vanity. (Ecclesiastes 3: 18-19)(NRSV)

By his own will he brought us into being through the word of truth, so that we should have first place among all his creatures. (James 1:18)(TEV)

As we have seen in the previous discussion, it is apparent that man is an animal, and what is more, he has evolved from animal ancestors, even the simplest of organisms, just as all of life has. This is a difficult concept for some Christians to accept because it seems to conflict with the pre-Christian biblical account of God creating man directly. However, the quote from Ecclesiastes (above) is also from the Old Testament and was included there for a reason—it held some great truth. Since God is the author of both the physical life and the Christian faith, God must be consistent with himself. It is our responsibility as Christians to find the ways in which our faith and our physical existence are mutually consistent and not seek to separate the two. As much as we would like to, we must not separate the creature from the creation.

Actually, the entire Old Testament supports the Ecclesiastes concept of the relationship between man and animals. They continually used animals as substitutes for humans in sacrifice. Leviticus says that *"the life of every living thing is its blood"* (Leviticus 17:14*b*)(NRSV), and shedding animal blood was a sufficient equivalent for human blood. A goat was used to bear the communal sins and sent off as the "scapegoat" into the desert to banish the evil from their midst (Leviticus 16:20-22).

The New Testament continues this understanding, and indeed, it is, as we shall see, among the fundamentals of Christianity. I see no conflict in the scriptures, but support throughout for an understanding of the animal-like nature of humans, and this idea explains many things about the origins of sin and suffering. More importantly, as we shall see in chapter 5, the Christian faith does not leave humans to live their lives as animals, even though very intelligent ones, but instead, elevates them beyond this world to a new level of existence.

We are animals without a doubt, and mammals to be more specific. Mammals that breathe, eat, sleep, urinate, defecate, and copulate, bear and suckle their young just like all other mammals in the world. If you forget this fact in the sophistication of our modern lives, just consider your body. Have you ever wondered why you have toenails? Nuisance things that always need cutting but don't have much use to us. They were useful to an ancient animal ancestor as he climbed high on some leafy branch. Toenails have come along for the ride, and maybe they serve some as protection for the toes, although it's not easy to be convinced of that after you have just stubbed your toe on the dresser leg. There must have been no advantage to get rid of them, so there they are.

Why do men have nipples? If God had created the first man from the dust and the first woman from his rib, why did men get nipples? Obviously, it is because we are a single creature and males are derived from the fundamental female organism by the presence of a recently discovered gene on the Y chromosome. This gene causes fetal hormonal changes that make minor structural changes and give us males. The nipples were left behind as reminder that males are actually derived from the female and can almost be transformed into females with high doses of the female hormone, estrogen.

Anyone who has had a baby or who has observed a baby being born must be assured of our animal nature. Actually most mammals make this a more facile process than our species does because to support our upright posture, we have a modified narrow pelvic bone structure that makes it hard for the baby to get through. During the whole delivery procedure, from the first contraction to the moment when the tiny wriggling human is expelled from her body, a mother's physical nature totally consumes her. It is anything but spiritual—and only the human mind in retrospect can make it into a spiritual experience.

We could go on and on, looking at appendixes, hairy chests, balding heads, and cellulite, all part of our animal bodies. Just because we give our bodies sophisticated treatments and adornments doesn't change the fact of our animal nature. Desmond Morris, in his best-selling book, *The Naked Ape*, gives a detailed description of just exactly how much of an animal we are. He points out that "we have arisen essentially as primate predators," and much of our behavior still reflects that heritage. It is his thesis that since we couldn't compete very well physically with the other predators, a vastly increased brainpower was needed. To accomplish this, we resorted to what was called *neotony*. *Neotony* means that we adopted infantile characteristics that would give us advantages as adults. These included a larger brain size relative to body size and loss of fur covering to give us better cooling during the chase of the hunt. In addition, the infant stage was greatly prolonged. All of these characteristics arose by selectively shutting off the genes that controlled adult development in our animal forbearers. Unfortunately, our sexual development raced on ahead of our mental development, and everyone is aware of the troubles that has caused us. There is little doubt that as Morris says,

> The fundamental patterns of behavior laid down in our early days as hunting apes still shine through all our affairs, no matter how lofty they may be. If the organization of our earthier activities—our feeding, our fear, our aggression, our sex, our parental care—had been developed solely by cultural means, there can be little doubt that we would have got it under better control by now, and twisted it this way and that to suit the increasingly extraordinary demands put upon it by our technological advances. But we have not done so. We have repeatedly bowed our heads before our animal nature and tacitly admitted the existence of the complex beast that stirs within us. If we are honest, we will confess that it will take millions of years, and the same genetic process of natural selection that put it there, to change it.

Yet we are different from the other animals. Our brains, our upright posture, and our opposable thumbs have put us quantum leaps ahead of our nearest mammalian competitors. Animals only rarely use tools and then in only rudimentary ways. They don't build anything very complex, and when they do, they act primarily by instinct for they do not plan very far ahead. Surely the beaver's pond is the most spectacular animal construction achievement. In only 30,000 years humans have moved from stone-tipped spears to hydrogen bombs, from caves to skyscrapers, from cave paintings to the Mona Lisa—all because of the power of their brains made for reasoning and their hands made for using tools.

Recent research has shown, however, that many animals, particularly our closest cousins, the chimpanzees, possess much more intelligence than we had previously ascribed to them, even to the point of rudimentary language abilities. Some chimpanzees and gorillas, who have been trained in a form of sign language, have put together unrelated language elements to create new thoughts. As impressive as these abilities are, the gap between humans and apes is still enormous and will never be bridged.

Although we have already talked about Adam and Eve in the Garden of Eden in relationship to the beginnings of civilization in the Mesopotamian delta, the story of the beautiful garden can also apply to our animal beginnings as Harold Kushner pointed out in his book, *When Bad Things Happen to Good People*. In the garden, man was in full harmony with God and with nature. Is not the animal existence fully in harmony with God? Animals only do what instinct and immediate need drive them to do. Some researchers feel that animal awareness is much like our dream state, which may be the animal portion of our brains asserting itself once the more powerful thinking part has shut down in sleep. In dreams there is no planning for the future or complicated philosophy; rather the mind reacts to events as they occur, not thinking much beyond the current stimulus. Similarly, animals simply adapt and relate to their environment. They rarely try to change or destroy it other than building nests or dens by an inherited pattern.

Animals may have rudimentary cognitive abilities, but everything they do is without malice or spite. Animals do not plot mischief or evil. There is no evil in them for they cannot reason right or wrong in a moral sense. They are also more violent than we naively believe. It has been shown that animals kill more of their own kind than we humans do, even with all of our terrible wars. Much of this killing derives from a primitive instinct to increase the likelihood that the strongest individual's genes will survive and be reproduced. It is the constant struggle of survival of the fittest. Animals do not kill for jealousy or hatred or meanness. They kill because at the moment that is what they were meant to do. No evil or immorality can be applied to it. Leslie Weatherhead in *The Christian Agnostic* used the following example to explain this:

> The fierce, hungry tiger seeks to end his hunger by attacking the gazelle for whom speed, touched off by fear, is the only hope for escape. No one can rightly use the word "cruel" about the tiger. Moral values do not exist. A strong tiger finds another feasting on a deer and drives the weaker tiger off the prey. This is not "stealing." Moral values are unknown. The tiger feels the urge of sex and seeks a mate. If he is strong enough, he may take a tigress, sought after, and already possessed by, another, and he copulates with her. At this stage of development "adultery," "lust," and "promiscuity" have no meaning.

To deny this lack of morality in animal behavior brings on the ludicrous efforts of the little old lady who wanted to diaper animals and who turned away in shock at the sight of animals mating. Fortunately, some of the excellent wildlife photography seen on television has not been subject to such ridiculous morality.

Thus, in a sense, when humans were still animals they were living in Eden. The "knowledge of good and evil" was not yet theirs. "He was naked and not ashamed" (Genesis 2:25). Humans depended upon God for all that they had. The earth was their beneficent garden.

Fundamentally, the Garden of Eden story has to do with man gaining knowledge. Although this was seemingly forbidden by God, it is this that separates humans from their animal cousins. Kushner spoke of this when he wrote,

> Like our almost-but-not-quite-human ancestors, animals eat from the Tree of Life; they eat and they run and they mate. But the Tree of Knowledge of Good and Evil is off limits to them.

The early writers of the Genesis story were well aware of the problems that having knowledge of good and evil had caused humanity. No other animal had such a problem. Animals could not do evil; they could only do what being an animal made them do. But humans, with their gift of intelligence, now felt cursed. No longer could they innocently depend on the natural bounty around them as the other animals did. Now that they had found that farming was a more reliable source of food, they were cursed to scrape the ground. When they found that other men's needs conflicted with their own, dissension, hatred, and even murder resulted.

Undoubtedly humanity's moral sense did not come in an instant and certainly did not come from eating the fruit of any special tree. It evolved slowly as did all of their physical abilities. However it came, it was a gift from God. It went hand in hand with their increased intellect, and this knowledge of good and evil was obviously just what God desired. It is this that makes humans in the "image of God." It is exactly this that God must have desired for his people—a natural outcome of human intelligence. It was not forbidden to his creature, but they were warned, because God was aware of the terrible cost that comes with the "knowledge of good and evil." He knew that it would place upon man the burden of choice. Were they ready to assume it?

Paul spoke to this in Romans where he wrote that the law, the codified knowledge of good and evil, was responsible for creating an awareness of sin.

> But it was the Law that made me know what sin is. If the Law had not said, "Do not desire what belongs to someone else," I would not have known such a desire. But by means of that commandment sin found its chance to stir up all kinds of selfish desires in me. Apart from the law, sin is a dead thing.(Romans 7:7b-8)(TEV)

God's warning to Adam not to eat the fruit of the tree of knowledge of good and evil clearly represents the fact that humans must be ready to accept the responsibilities that such knowledge entails before they so eagerly eat of the tree. For by eating of this fruit, the animal adam becomes the man Adam. He is now fully created in the "image of God." And it is this knowledge that ultimately separated him from the animals.

The Difference between Bad and Evil

Before we proceed, it is important to understand that there is a difference between the words "bad" and "evil," even though the English language often uses the words interchangeably. Knowledge of evil is not the same as knowledge of what is bad. Animals know and experience may things that are bad: storms, cold, predators, anything that threatens their well-being and survival. Only humans know what evil is: willful malevolence toward their fellow human for their own advantage or not—greed, lust, hate—only man knows it all. Human intelligence, when combined with ancient animal instinct for survival, created evil. Humans no longer lived in harmony with God, nature, or their fellow humans. The mind of humans—still abounding in their animal drives and passions, still very much just intelligent animals—twisted their instincts into willful malevolence. Sin was born. Is this not the best explanation of the now somewhat neglected doctrine of original sin? We are sinners because we were born as animals, but with the capacity to rebel against our creator, God.

Morality probably began with the tribal taboos that made it possible for small groups and clans to survive in the hostile environment. But when the animals-called-humans became civilized and began to live in communities and eventually cities, the morality became law. Civilization allowed people to become specialized, and when they no longer had to struggle every day just to find food, there was much more freedom to philosophize. The first religions were polytheistic, evolving from the original animistic worship of the sun and moon, of storms and tides, rocks, seas, and animals and trees, earthquakes and volcanoes. The belief that each of these possessed a spirit that could be appeased made some manner of control over nature possible. Science has replaced this ancient animism with our modern, more rational means to attempt control of nature.

From this early polytheism, there developed, principally among the nomadic tribes called the Hebrews, an understanding that there was a single supernatural God who maintained a supernatural set of moral laws which he revealed to his chosen people. This, of course, is the Jewish foundation of our Christian faith. The description of God's revelation of his nature and his laws to humanity and humankind's response to them is the story of the Old Testament. Humans had emerged from their animal nature, once responding only to the forces of the physical universe, to become creatures who now were responding to the forces from the spiritual universe.

New Testament Concepts

Does the Bible really refer to humans as animals? Is this a New Testament concept or is this just a twisted interpretation of the scriptures?

Paul described different kinds of flesh for humans and animals:

> Not all flesh is alike, but there is one flesh for human beings, another for animals, another for birds, and another for fish. (1 Corinthians 15:39)(NRSV)

He, of course, did not know anything about the modern science of genetics and immunology. Individual species of animals are indeed unique types of "flesh" that cannot interbreed. Modern organ transplants have made it clear that human tissue (except blood) cannot even be shared by individuals of the same species without the immune system launching an all-out attempt to reject it. Even blood must be carefully typed before it can be used. Organ transplants are only possible with the use of drugs that suppress the immune response. Yet, the fundamental biochemistry of all animals is remarkably similar, and mapping the amino-acid sequences in some of the major enzymes common to all creatures reveals that we are very closely related.

The Old Testament writers sensed that humans were just another version of the animals. The writer of Ecclesiastes certainly did. He recognized that we were all sharing the same fate—death. Many people ignore this less familiar passage and emphasize the Genesis story which they have been taught from childhood. So strong is the concept of a unique creation for humans, that the Scopes trial was fought because of it.

One finds that whenever the words "flesh, worldly or natural self" are used in the Bible, they can be translated in the sense of the "animal body, the animal nature of humans, human being, or human nature," meaning not "spiritual." The term "human being" is not used to mean something exalted; it is always used in contrast to our spiritual nature, and it is evident that the concept is prevalent throughout the Bible. In support of this, we find that Today's English Version (*TEV*) often translates the "flesh" of the King James and New Revised Standard Versions as "human being." (*Italics are mine*)

> Jesus said, "The spirit indeed is willing, but the *flesh* is weak" (Matthew 26:41*b*)(NRSV)

> "And the Word became *flesh* and lived among us" (John 1:14*a*)(NRSV), i.e., the Word became a *human being* and, full of grace and truth, lived among us (John 1:14*a*)(*TEV*).

> While we were living in the *flesh,* our sinful passions, aroused by the law, were at work in our members to bear fruit for death (Romans 7:5)(NRSV), i.e., for when we lived according to our *human nature*, the sinful desires stirred up by the Law were at work in our bodies, and we were useful in the service of death. (Romans 7:5)(TEV)

Peter doesn't even require the translation,

> But these people, however, are like irrational *animals,* mere
> creatures of instinct, born to be caught and killed. They
> slander what they do not understand, and when those
> creatures are destroyed, they also will be destroyed, suffering
> the penalty for doing wrong.(2 Peter 2:12-13*b*)(NRSV)

Peter was undoubtedly talking about the "false prophets" of
his day—and ours, but it applies to anyone who lives by
uncontrolled animal passions.

Paul continues the discussion,

> What *human nature* does is quite plain. It shows itself in
> immoral, filthy, and indecent actions; in worship of idols
> and witchcraft. People become enemies and they fight; they
> become jealous, anxious and ambitious. They separate into
> parties and groups; they are envious, get drunk, have orgies,
> and do other things like these. (Galatians 5:19-21*b*)(TEV)

> You must put to death, then the *earthly* desires at work
> in you, such as sexual immorality, indecency, lust, evil
> passions, and greed (for greed is a form of idolatry).
> Because of such things God's anger will come upon those
> who do not obey him. At one time you yourselves used
> to live according to such desires, when your life was
> dominated by them.
>
> But now you must get rid of all these things: anger,
> passion, and hateful feelings. No insults or obscene talk
> must ever come from your lips. Do not lie to one another, for
> you have put off the old self with its habits and have put on
> the new self. (Colossians 3:5-10*a*)(TEV)

These are only a few of the possible examples. In chapter 5 we
shall see God's solution to the problem that our animal nature,
our flesh, causes us.

So Where Does the Devil Fit In?

Before we leave this discussion, we must talk about the devil or Satan. If we ascribe all sin to the expression of our animal nature and passions, where does the devil come in? Jesus certainly considered him as the power of evil. Still, the Old Testament never blamed Satan for any of the failures or sins of man. All blame was squarely on the shoulders of the human perpetrators or even God. Where was the devil to take responsibility? It turns out that the concept of an evil supernatural power did not come into Hebrew theology until the Babylonian exile in the period 587-539 BC and the subsequent restoration by the Persians. The Persians, who had two deities representing good or evil, were admired by the returning Jews. Supported by Babylonian and Greek influences, this concept of an evil power was adopted into Judaism as the idea of Satan.

Whether Satan is an actual spiritual universe entity, opposed to God and inspiring evil in humans, or simply the personification of all the evil within human beings and their society, has been debated for a long time. Isn't the medieval image of the devil, resplendent with horns and hooves of a goat and outfitted with a serpent's tail, a symbolic portrayal of our animal nature as the source of all evil? I think that the earlier humans sensed they were animals more than moderns do, and it is only our modern sophistication that falsely leads us into thinking we are something different. It is especially here that science can help theology with new understanding, for the evidence of evolution and of humans as animals seems totally sufficient to explain the presence of sin in the world, without invoking the Persian god of evil. As Weatherhead wrote:

> Many do not regard this view of sin's origin as adequate, but for myself I cannot think of any form of human sin which cannot be traced back to the entail of our animal ancestry to which has been added the terrible additions of the power of the human imagination . . .

Humans, as intelligent animals, must bear the cost of life in terms of suffering. Because we think—we suffer—and we suffer more acutely than animals ever can. Theology has struggled to explain it, but suffering, by whatever source, is part of our physical life, not our spiritual life. We shall see what our evolutionary creation says to us about suffering in the next chapter.

What Is to Become of Us?

We cannot leave the subject of human beings and their animal origins without looking at their future. If we humans, the human animals, are a product of billions of years of evolution, what is in store for us? Will we continue to evolve? Since species remain stable, sometimes for millions of years, we may change very little. Will it be as Morris said?

> So there he stands, our vertical, hunting, weapon-toting, territorial, neotenous, brainy Naked Ape, a primate by ancestry and a carnivore by adoption, ready to conquer the world. But he is a very new and experimental departure and new models frequently have imperfections. For him the main troubles will stem from the fact that his culturally operated advances will race ahead of any further genetic ones. His genes will lag behind, and he will be constantly reminded that, for all his environment-molding achievements, he is still at heart a very naked ape.

Or will it be as some people think? Human technology may be the route of any further human evolution, and biological evolution will play a role no more. Hans Moravec of the Carnegie Mellon University suggests that humans will become immortal by becoming bionic. More and more of their body organs will be replaced by mechanical substitutes as they wear out. Their brains will eventually become computer assisted by insertion of tiny computers so that the computer's thoughts will seem like their own. Finally their entire personalities will be digitized onto a computer, and they will have become immortal by becoming a machine.

The question remains: Is humanity capable of handling immortality? Not until they have solved the problem of sin and evil would this even be desirable. Even if they can achieve immortality by use of technology, this will be a physical-world immortality, and their feet of clay, even if they are now robotic feet, will still be stuck in the physical universe.

The good news of Christianity does not leave humanity as animals or even robots. Instead, a new route of evolution is presented to us. The Gospel of Jesus Christ proclaims an open invitation to human beings to evolve beyond the physical universe and become inhabitants of the spiritual universe. Humans need not remain bound to the realm of matter and space; they can access the realm of utter reality and power. It is only there that immortality can have any real meaning.

CHAPTER FOUR

WHY SUFFERING?

But ask the animals, and they will teach you;
the birds of the air and they will tell you;
ask the plants of the earth, and they will teach you;
and the fish of the sea will declare to you.
Who among all these does not know
that the hand of the Lord has done this?
In this hand is the life of every living thing
and the breath of every human being.
(Job 12:7-10)(NRSV)

We are animals indeed, and as animals we suffer, perhaps not in the same way as other animals, but often more acutely. What is this burden that our existence on earth brings to us? Next to death, itself, suffering is the major difficulty humanity faces. Sin is the primary problem that God has with us, but undoubtedly, suffering is the primary problem that we have with God. Suffering can make or break a person of faith, and theologians have struggled for millennia to come up with a satisfactory explanation for the untold suffering in the world.

The Bible appears equally frustrated, for the major biblical sufferer, Job was given no explanation, only more suffering. His friends had quickly come to the rationale that he must have sinned greatly, and this suffering (as was commonly believed in Old Testament times) was his just punishment for sin. But Job was a man of God, and since he knew he had not sinned, that reason was not valid. Perhaps his real problem was his lack of moral humility.

Although Job would not give up his faith in the goodness of God, even God gave no explanation for his suffering or the presence of suffering in the world. He simply told Job that it was not for him to understand, because that was the way he made the world.

Even the New Testament fails to give us a basis for the presence of suffering. Some people that Jesus healed, such as the man let down through the roof on the pallet by his friends, were told that their sins were forgiven, but this seems to be an act of encouragement rather than an explanation for the suffering or the means by which healing was accomplished. Several other people were healed with no reference to sin and forgiveness. Jesus said, when challenged,

> Why do you raise such questions in your hearts? Which is easier to say to the paralytic, "Your sins are forgiven," or to say, "Stand up and take your mat and walk"? (Mark 2:8-9)(NRSV)

He appeared to be using it simply as something to encourage the man, for the healing had already occurred. Other people were healed when he admonished evil spirits and demons to depart the suffering victim. Indeed, evil spirits and demons were commonly believed to be the cause of much illness in that day, particularly mental illness. Most of the symptoms described have more rational explanations today. However, the usual healing statement that Jesus made was simply, "Your faith has made you well; go in peace or be healed of your disease." No blame or rationale for the suffering was delivered; just encouragement and healing, for it wasn't Jesus's role to explain, but to heal and save.

The Three Types of Suffering

As we continue our discussion of suffering, we must be clear about the three types of suffering that we experience. Their causes are varied and their results are different, so they must be understood for what they are.

The first cause of much suffering in the world today is because we sin. The Old Testament theologians were right—sin causes suffering. It is not the cause of all suffering, but it causes a lot. Our failure to follow God's rules for living life very often leads to disaster. Whether our sin varies from self-indulgence all the way to serious criminal activity, either our bodies or our society will react and cause us trouble. Although, I may not be politically correct in saying so, much of the AIDS epidemic is due to sin against the rules God has established in the physical universe for monogamous, healthy, reproductive, and loving sexuality. Promiscuity has always been dangerous. If we rail against the unfairness of it, it is because we refuse to accept the rules God has established for successful living in his world. His rules were lovingly made for our benefit and good health, never for our punishment and slavery.

Usually we can understand suffering that is due to our sin, even if we don't like it, for it has an obvious cause-and-effect rationale. It is acceptable because we accept the concept of punishment for wrongdoing. But God is not the initiator of the suffering, and this Jesus carefully noted.

At that very time there were some present who told him about the Galileans whose blood Pilate had mingled with their sacrifices. He asked them, "Do you think that because these Galileans suffered in this way they were worse sinners than all other Galileans? No, I tell you; but unless you repent, you will all perish as they did. Or the eighteen who were killed when the tower of Siloam fell on them—do you think that they were worse offenders than all others living in Jerusalem? No, I tell you; but unless you repent, you will all perish just as they did." (Luke 13:1-5)(NRSV)

As he walked along, he saw a man blind form birth. His disciples asked him, "Rabbi, who sinned, this man or his parents, that he was born blind?" Jesus answered, "Neither this man nor his parents sinned; he was born blind so that God's works might be revealed in him." (John 9:1-3)(NRSV)

God treats the just and the unjust with the same loving concern:

> For he makes his sun rise on the evil and on the good, and
> sends rain on the righteous and on the unrighteous.
> (Matthew 5:45*b*)(NRSV)

It is the physical universe forces that usually suffice to nail the sinner. You cannot long mistreat your body and not pay the price in ill health. Our cemeteries full of lung cancer victims and drunk drivers attest to that. You cannot long mistreat your fellow human either and get away with it. We still fight long and costly wars trying to teach that lesson. When the physical universe doesn't strike back, as seems to happen sometimes when the vilest of men leads a long and prosperous life, death evens the score and entry into the spiritual realm is blocked; his life ceases in the same way as all other animals cease to exist. As the New Testament says,

> They also will be destroyed, suffering the penalty for doing
> wrong." (2 Peter 2:12*b*-13*a*)(NRSV)

> For the wages of sin is death. (Romans 6:23*a*)(NRSV)

A second type of suffering is also easy to comprehend, for it is the suffering we experience because of our service to God. Jesus' suffering is the best example of this. He did not suffer because he had sinned, but because other people sinned and killed him. This type of suffering (because of the sin of others) is of such great power that it can redeem the entire human race. Already it has forever changed the course of history. God does not will this type of suffering, because he does not will people to commit sin one against the other, but it is within his will that his people suffer it, for he transforms it into works of grace. As Peter said:

> If you endure when you are beaten for doing wrong, what
> credit is that? But if you endure when you do right and
> suffer for it, you have God's approval. For to this you have

been called, because Christ also suffered for you, leaving you an example, so that you should follow in his steps. He committed no sin; no deceit was found in his mouth. When he was abused, he did not return abuse; when he suffered, he did not threaten; but he entrusted himself to the one who judges justly. He himself bore our sins in this body on the cross, so that, free from sins, we might live for righteousness; by his wounds you have been healed. For you were going astray like sheep, but now you have returned to the shepherd and guardian of your souls.(1 Peter 2:20-25)(NRSV)

The third type of suffering is the suffering that comes to us for no reason at all. There is much suffering that cannot be traced to sin—suffering that just happens to us. Accidents, cancer, birth defects, heart attacks, Alzheimer's disease, muscular dystrophy, earthquakes, floods, tornadoes, and hurricanes are just a few. Even though these tragedies are known to have underlying causes and sometimes might be attributed to someone's mistakes or sin, most have no known cause. Still they leave innocent victims, scattered and miserable, in their wake. Automobile accidents leave thousands of innocent people dead or critically injured and incapacitated for the rest of their lives. Many thousands will suffer the agony of severe memory loss at the onset of Alzheimer's disease, causing extraordinary care and financial burdens on their families. Cancer strikes for no apparent reason, leaving untold suffering, death, and sorrow.

The problem with this type of suffering is that we are still impotent to know exactly where and when it will strike. Some smokers who have had the habit all of their adult lives will live to be in their nineties, while others will die young. Tornadoes and earthquakes strike randomly and people survive or are killed and injured in no logical manner. There is no reason for the way such suffering strikes. My brother died of cancer at age forty-eight. He neither smoked nor drank and was, I believe, a good Christian. I was a chemist and worked with toxic, carcinogenic, and radioactive chemicals for many years, but I have outlived him. Life just isn't fair.

"It's God's will," is still the feeble comfort that will be offered by most Christians today. The mistake they make is to associate unexplained suffering with the suffering incurred in service to God. Certainly, we cannot equate the suffering due to illness with the suffering that God allowed for his Son on Calvary. That suffering had a purpose and was willingly accepted by our loving Savior. Christian suffering in God's service is creative, loving, and within God's will. Cancer has no purpose except to kill us and is never willingly chosen. If God had willed these diseases and sufferings upon people as the Old Testament taught, then Jesus and our medical profession could be accused of thwarting God's will by healing them. This, obviously, cannot be the case, because Jesus taught us God gives good gifts to his children (Matthew 7:11). How then can we explain our undeserved suffering as being God's will? Is it our lot in life to stoically accept the misery as Job did, and love God anyway, even if he brought this suffering upon us? As Harold Kushner wrote:

> I can worship a God who hates suffering but cannot eliminate it, more easily than I can worship a God who chooses to make children suffer and die, for whatever exalted reason.

Jesus spoke of a God who cares deeply for us and seeks to keep us whole. He must hate such suffering and share it with us. Again, Kushner explains:

> God does not cause our misfortunes. Some are caused by bad luck, some are caused by bad people, and some are simply an inevitable consequence of our being human and being mortal, living in a world of inflexible natural laws. The painful things that happen to us are not punishments for our misbehavior, nor are they in any way part of some grand design on God's part. Because the tragedy is not God's will, we need not feel hurt or betrayed by God when tragedy strikes. We can turn to Him in overcoming it, precisely because we can tell ourselves that God is as outraged by it as we are.

God cannot will suffering on us and then seek to heal us. That doesn't seem consistent, even to the human mind. When Jesus discussed the sparrows and said,

> Yet not one of them will fall to the ground apart from your Father, (Matthew 10:29*b*)(NRSV)

he was not saying that God willed the sparrow to fall, but that no sparrow will fall without his concern and knowledge. It is within God's will that illness, suffering, and tragedy occur in this world, because that is the way he made it, and perhaps the only way that he could make it. He does not will that any specific tragedy befall an individual.

If God doesn't will it or cause it as part of some mysterious "grand design," how then do we ultimately explain suffering? As long as we look at human beings as a separate creation, unlike other creatures of the world, we will not find the answer. Here modern science in the theory of evolution can serve the theologian well.

Undeserved random suffering is not explainable from a spiritual point of view. For such suffering is a physical-world phenomenon, and its roots are in the physical universe. It is only the discovery of evolution as God's method of creation of living forms that gives a rational explanation for the presence of suffering in the world. "Why would God allow this to happen to me?" is the question we all ask when suffering strikes. Clearly, our animal nature derived from our evolution explains that we must suffer injury and illness and die as all our fellow animals do.

How else are we to explain the presence of cancer and birth defects and other diseases that plague our species and many others? If God created everything just as it is today, as some creationists claim, why did he create disease? Don't we have enough problems with evil? Why did he create defects in our life systems, such as in our birth process? No one looking at a deformed child can rightly call it a gift from God. God surely wants all children to be healthy and normal. The evolutionary origin of our species is the only rational explanation of this tragic phenomenon. Such defects are necessarily present in the beautiful, but extremely complicated, system called life. Our animal cousins experience the same imperfections, but these offspring are doomed to quickly die in the harsh animal world, just as quickly forgotten, and rarely mourned. Only humans, largely because of the respect and value ascribed to human life by the revealed love of God, have relentlessly sought to maintain lives, even of deformed but viable children, as well we should. These and all of our physical sufferings are not sent to us as the will of a cruel God, but are the result of our evolutionary animal origins. We suffer more because we think more, but we share the difficulties with all life that has come before us.

Death is a required part of the survival-of-the-fittest method for designing creatures, each perfectly adapted to their environment. There are only limited resources to use as food and shelter, and in the animal world, only the strongest are given the right to survive and reproduce in order that the species might flourish. Any other way would lead to destruction for all. It was God's original and still perfect design. If animals die, then humans, as animals, must die too. The difference is as Kushner wrote,

> All living creatures are fated to die, but only humans know it.

God does not will disease, injury, and death on animals or people; rather it is the nature of the hazards of the environment and sometimes the parasitic organisms that have co-evolved to prey on them. Humans, viewing it all from the top of the heap, rarely have to experience the terror of being pursued by a predator, but for our animal cousins, this is a real fact of life, and often we are the predator. We have eliminated most of the other animal threats to our safety, but still struggle with our fellow human beings, microorganisms, viruses, and cellular malfunctions like cancer.

A few years ago, a lovely lady in our church died of cancer at age forty-nine, leaving her husband and four grown children. She was an inspiration and joy to all of us who knew her, and she is missed by her family and friends. I suppose many people have comforted themselves and the family by saying that her death was God's will. Perhaps it was, but only at the point where cancer had so ravaged her body that our merciful God willed she be released from life and its pain and suffering. But it was not God's will that she had cancer. The God that Jesus revealed to us does not will cancer on anyone. Instead, he suffers when this happens to one of his children. He needed her here, just as her husband and her children needed her—just as her new grandson needed to grow up knowing his grandmother.

We immediately ask, why didn't God heal her? Why didn't God get rid of the cancer? But he replies, "I gave you three things to heal. I gave you bodies that are built to heal themselves, I gave you brains for science to give you medicine and healing, and I gave you faith in me that sustains the other two." I'm sure he tried by what spiritual means he has available to him, such as stimulating the natural healing processes within her body and by giving strength and wisdom to her doctors. The only way that God can eliminate cancer is to eliminate life altogether. Actually, healing cancer is really our responsibility, not his. God gave humans dominion or responsibility over the world, and since cancer is a problem of this world, it is our task to solve it. He has no hands to build X-ray machines; he has no hands to cut out tumors or to develop new forms of chemotherapy.

When our grief makes us want to curse the injustice of it all, we must curse our ignorance—our wasteful use of enormous resources to engineer the means to destroy lives rather than to heal lives. We must curse all the money we waste on destructive drugs and alcohol in futile efforts to numb our lives rather than to save them. It certainly isn't right to curse God.

My friend knew that there is much more to life than what we experience in this world. Her strength and courage witnessed to the strength God gave her as she faced the hand life had unfairly dealt her. Her strength can be our strength—strength to continue to live a life devoted to God, for God wills that we live abundantly as she did, no matter what we have to face, for he is with us.

There can be no doubt that science has done more than any other human function to reduce the pain, suffering, and death in our species. Those of us who lived through the conquering of smallpox, polio, measles, and many other diseases can appreciate the tremendous good that medical science has done. Our hope for future health improvements must remain in the physical-universe gift of science given to us by God for solving our physical-universe problems.

As Christians we are only asked to faithfully accept God's love, we are not asked to hopelessly bear suffering. We are encouraged to fight disease and suffering with all of our resources. God gives us strength and faith along with the help of medical science to overcome it for he knows our suffering—indeed, he experiences it with us. Because of God's loving support, we can unite with Paul when he said,

> And not only that, but we also boast in our sufferings, knowing that suffering produces endurance, and endurance produces character, and character produces hope, and hope does not disappoint us, because God's love has been poured into our hearts through the Holy Spirit that has been given to us. (Romans 5:3-5)(NRSV)

Have you ever, in this life, seen endurance and character developed by meekly accepting the troubles of life as your just punishment, God's will, or your lot in life? Endurance and character are developed by struggle and achievement against the odds thrown against us. There is no doubt that these spiritual universe traits are developed in this physical world by just these troubles. I have to believe that is why we begin as animals. With God on our side, we have all the strength we need to face life in the physical world as it really is. Our hope sustains us because God has promised that there is more to life than what we experience here as human animals. He has shown us a way to grow beyond our animal existence, to become what God intends for all his children—to become more than human.

CHAPTER FIVE

MORE THAN HUMAN

See what love the Father has given us, that we should be called the children of God; and that us what we are. The reason the world does not know us is that it did not know him. Beloved, we are God's children now; what we will be has not yet been revealed. What we do know is this: when he is revealed, we will be like him, for we will see him as he is. (1 John 3:1-2)(NRSV)

Is existence as an intelligent animal the end of the line for us? Is that all there is? Are we doomed to be born, to live some few short years, and to die as all our animal cousins die? Modern science can only answer yes to those questions. Any other answer would conjure up further questions that cannot be answered by applying the scientific method. To answer these questions would require study of the spiritual universe, and science is unable to enter there. Instead, the spiritual universe must be approached by faith, and for that, we must go to our principle source of faith information, the Bible.

In the revelation of God that Jesus presents to us in the New Testament, we find a new dimension added to our existence in the physical universe—access to the spiritual universe. (I like to use the word "universe" rather than "world" because it points out the vastness and completeness of the spiritual realm.) The word most often used in the New Testament for the spiritual universe is "heaven," but the authors of the Gospels wrote that Jesus also use the terms "the Kingdom of God," or "eternal life." Paul explained the spiritual universe to the Corinthians using the metaphor of a tent and a house.

For we know that when this tent we live in—our body here
on earth—is torn down, God will have house in heaven for
us to live in, a home he himself has made, which will last
forever. And now we sigh, so great is our desire that our
home which comes from heaven should be put on over us;
by being clothed with it we shall not be without a body.
While we live in this earthly tent, we groan with a feeling of
oppression; it is not that we want to get rid of our earthly
body, but that we want to have the heavenly one put on
over us, so that what is mortal will be transformed by life.
God is the one who has prepared us for this change, and he
gave us his Spirit as the guarantee of all that he has in store
for us.

So we are always full of courage. We know that as long
as we are at home in the body we are away from the Lord's
home. For our life is a matter of faith, not of sight. We are
full of courage and would much prefer to leave our home in
the body and be at home with the Lord. More than anything
else, however, we want to please him, whether in our home
here or there. (2 Corinthians 5:1-9)(TEV)

As Paul points out, we are only partial citizens of the real
universe as long as we are animals bound to the physical world
with no escape. God would have us become citizens of the whole
universe, spiritual and physical, realizing as Paul did, the limitations
of our physical bodies. Only when we are eventually freed of our
physical universe bonds will we be able to fully experience the
spiritual realm.

As we discussed in the third chapter, the concept of man as an
intelligent animal that has evolved through millennia—a creature
of the earth and for the earth, intelligent but in conflict with his
animal nature—is in no way contrary to the biblical idea of man,
the sinner. In fact, it explains how the top creature in God's creation
could be such a big sinner, in contrast to the goodness of creation.
I think that science has found the answer for us by revealing the
evolutionary creation that God used. The theory of evolution has

clearly provided one of the answers to the theological problem of the origin of sin in a creation God saw as "good."

But science is powerless to solve the problem of sin, because sin is breaking the rules of the spiritual universe not rules of the physical universe. Science usually avoids the problem by suggesting sin doesn't exist since it cannot determine that the spiritual universe exists. It is our animal passions in conflict with the spiritual universe rules that get us into spiritual trouble. Humans have set up some rules to govern civilization that are a combination of physical world rules and spiritual universe rules. Indeed, Earl Wilson once said that we have thirty-five million laws trying to enforce ten commandments. But we sin only when we break the spiritual universe rules. When we break the physical world rules, we either get hurt or we "break the law."

If you attempt to walk across an open manhole, and you fall in, you have not committed a sin, you have merely tried to break the law of gravity. If you get a traffic ticket, you have not broken God's law but the law of man. If you curse your neighbor for some insult, you have sinned, but only if you burn his house down do you also have to face the world's laws. If you succumb to your natural passions and lust after someone of the opposite sex, you have not broken a law of man, but you have broken a spiritual law of God—you have sinned. If you have mutually willing sex with that person who is not your spouse, you have not broken a law (at least not one that can be enforced), but you have sinned. If you rape that person, you have broken laws in both universes, a government law and God's law, and thus you have sinned.

So it is apparent that the rules of the spiritual universe apply as much to our thoughts as to our actions, because God knows very well that our words and actions come from our thoughts. Jesus was quite clear about this in the Sermon on the Mount. He also said,

> Do you not see that whatever goes into the mouth enters the stomach, and goes out into the sewer? But what comes out of the mouth proceeds from the heart, and this is what

> defiles. For out of the heart come evil intentions, murder,
> adultery, fornication, theft, false witness, slander. These are
> what defile a person. (Matthew 15:17-20*a*)(NRSV)

The physical world has no way to punish us for our thoughts, so the physical world must wait until our sinful thoughts have turned to words or action. It is then that sin has its effect on our world. Although sin causes serious problems for the physical world because it destroys our relationships with each other, and the physical world may react to it, sin can only be healed from the spiritual universe. Only God is able to resolve it.

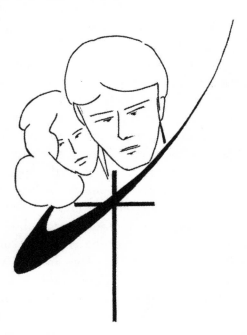

God's Solution to Sin

In his great love for his creation, God acted within his natural laws and raise up a son, a teacher, an example, a savior. "But," you will immediately object, "how can you say that he used natural law in the virgin birth of Jesus?" As with much of the working of the spiritual universe, we will never know how it happened. Maybe he simply acted by using natural circumstances in some unnoticed way as he usually does. (See chapter 6 for a fuller explanation of this.) Also possible is that he projected spiritual universe forces into the physical world and a woman conceived. (We will discuss this further in chapter 8.) Simply put, as Christians, we believe that God in some way caused Mary's conception. However it happened, whether by natural means or by supernatural means, is really not important. What is important is that in the birth of Jesus, God accomplished the profoundest change in human history ever experienced. And Jesus' birth and his growth and development into a man were completely natural in every other respect. God did not act in an ultra-natural way such as by dropping Jesus full-grown out of a cloud.

Through Jesus, God has given his intelligent animal a means by which to control sin and to enter into the spiritual universe and share in its power and eternity. This is the basic principal behind all of Jesus' life and teaching and all of Paul's preaching. It is the underlying concept of the "new birth," the "Kingdom of God," and "eternal life."

Although John 3:16 is said to be the Gospel in one sentence, John 1:12-13 is the reason for the Gospel.

> But to all who received him, who believed in his name, he gave power to become children of God: who were born, not of blood or of the will of the flesh or the will of man, but of God. (NRSV).

This is so important that we should hear it from Today's English Version (TEV) so that it is well understood.

> Some, however, did receive him and believed in him; so he gave them the right to become God's children. They did not become God's children by natural means, that is by being born as the children of a human father; God himself was their father.

A new level of existence is revealed here. We intelligent animals of the species *Homo sapiens sapiens*, we human beings, have an opportunity to be more than children of human parents—we can become the "children of God." In a sense we are all God's children because he is our Creator Father. But that is not the sense that the New Testament uses for the concept of "the children of God." This term is the one used to describe those of God's creatures, the highly intelligent animals called human beings, who have become citizens of the spiritual universe and no longer just inhabitants of the physical universe.

Indeed, Jesus used the animal concept of birth to describe becoming a new spiritual creature. All mammals like ourselves must be born, having grown in the womb in a sack of water, the amniotic fluid. But hear what Jesus said to Nicodemus:

> "I am telling you the truth: no one can see the Kingdom of God unless he is born again."
>
> "How can a grown man be born again?" Nicodemus asked. "He certainly cannot enter his mother's womb and be born a second time!"
>
> "I am telling you the truth," replied Jesus, "that no one can enter the Kingdom of God unless he is born of water and the Spirit. A person is born physically of human parents, but he is born spiritually of the Spirit. Do not be surprised because I tell you that you must be born again." (John 3:3-7)(TEV)

Baptism may be interpreted to represent the new birth in the spirit by reenacting the original birth from our mother's womb, in addition to the sense of cleansing from sin that the anointing with water symbolizes. The act of baptism, in itself, does not have any spiritual saving powers. It only represents the redeeming change that has taken place in one's life. We must be born as physical beings to live on this earth in the physical universe, and we must be born as spiritual beings to live in the spiritual universe.

To develop the analogy further, we might imagine that when we are born physically, we are given an embryonic spiritual nature, conceived by the Spirit of God. Unless this spirit is born to become an independent entity, free of dominance by the physical nature, it will die when the body dies and be no more, just as the fetus will die when trapped unborn in the womb of its mother. But if we are born as free and independent spiritual beings, we will live on when our physical nature dies.

> What I mean, brothers, is that what is made of flesh and blood cannot share in God's kingdom, and what is mortal cannot possess immortality. (1 Corinthians 15:50)(TEV)

Our spiritual being (soul) is still restricted to the space enclosed within our minds, since it must use our senses to communicate with the physical world, but it is now already a creature of the spiritual universe and can commune with the spiritual universe. The new-born "child of God" is directed to more and more subjugate his or her physical nature to his or her spiritual nature, until there is no difference. Such perfection may never be reached, but it is the ultimate goal. Our living spirit has been made now fully acceptable and sinless to God as his gift of grace, because of the sacrifice Jesus made for us by dying on the cross. This is how we can know we are a creature of the spiritual universe and yet honestly realize that we are still sinners. The degree to which we are able to control our physical, animal nature by our spiritual nature determines the level of our perfection from sin, our righteousness. But we do not earn this gift of God by our righteousness; our righteousness is the evidence that we are growing as spiritual beings. Without this growth, our spirits can wither and die.

God's Child

Our physical nature is declared by the Bible and confirmed by science to be a child of human parents and the physical world created by God. Our spiritual nature, being a "child of God," is not of the physical world although it still is in it. It is spirit, born of the Spirit of God and destined to live in the spiritual universe.

How then are we born of the Spirit, as Jesus insisted that we must be in order to inhabit the spiritual universe? By simply believing that Jesus was God's son, sent to us to save us from entrapment in the physical universe.

> For God so loved the world that he gave his only Son, so that everyone who believes in him may not perish but may have eternal life. Indeed, God did not send the Son into the world to condemn the world, but in order that the world might be saved through him. (John 3:16-17)(NRSV)

This is so simple that it is hard to believe it can be sufficient. But that is God's promise. Merely believe and he will give his Holy Spirit to you as a birthday gift. Unfortunately religious people who don't really believe it themselves have been putting additional rules in the way. But just like growing physically and mentally is the hard part of physical living, growing in the spirit is the hard part of being born spiritually. The hard part is putting our newborn spiritual nature in domination over our well-entrenched and dominant physical nature which is very strong and well established in our existence. Our spiritual nature must grow and develop by experiencing the trials and tribulations, the sorrows and joys of this world within our physical bodies, until it can become the controlling force in our lives. In this too, we have help. The very Spirit of God is living in us, nurturing and guiding our spiritual nature if we but submit to its leading. Then we can step forth as mature beings, serving freely the God who created us.

Paul speaks of this in Romans 8:3 (I am quoting from the TEV because they have translated the King James "flesh" to "human nature" for me.)

> What the Law could not do, because human nature was weak, God did. He condemned sin in human nature by sending his own Son, who came with a nature like man's sinful nature, to do away with sin. God did this so that the righteous demands of the Law might be fully satisfied in us

who live according to the Spirit, not according to human nature. Those who live as their human nature tells them to, have their minds controlled by what human nature wants. Those who live as the Spirit tells them to, have their minds controlled by what the Spirit wants. To be controlled by human nature results in death; to be controlled by the Spirit results in life and peace. And so a person becomes an enemy of God when he is controlled by his human nature; for he does not obey God's law and in fact cannot obey it. Those who obey their human nature cannot please God. (Romans 8:3-8)(TEV)

Just what then is the difference between a human being and a child of God? In our day and age, we have come to look on that which makes us truly human as the highest ideal for man to achieve. This is largely due, I confess, to the development of science and the power of human wisdom on its own, or so it appears, to greatly improve the lot of man. But the flaw in "humanism" is that it is firmly planted in the physical existence. Human beings will go on eternally struggling with their animal nature. As long as we live on this earth, our animal nature is still a part of us. We must breathe and eat and sleep. We must also accept the presence of our survival instincts, our sexual drives, and our hunger for material possessions and comfort. We must accept them, but we must let our new spiritual nature control them. The apostle Paul struggled with this problem.

For we know that the law is spiritual; but I am of the flesh, sold into slavery under sin. I do not understand my own actions. For I do not do what I want, but I do the very thing I hate. Now if I do what I do not want, I agree that the law is good. But in fact it is no longer I that do it, but sin that dwells within me. For I know that nothing good dwells within me, that is in my flesh. I can will what is right, but I cannot do it. For I do not do the good I want, but the evil I do not want is what I do. Now if I do what I do not want, it is no longer I that do it, but sin that dwells within me. (Romans 7:14-20)(NRSV)

The rewards of citizenship in the spiritual universe are so fantastic that the cost is cheap by comparison. As Jesus said:

> The Kingdom of Heaven [spiritual universe] is like this. A man happens to find a treasure hidden in a field. He covers it up again, and is so happy that he goes and sells everything he has, and then goes back and buys that field. (Matthew 13:44)(TEV)

> Also, the Kingdom of heaven is like this. A man is looking for fine pearls, and when he finds one that is unusually fine, he goes and sells everything he has, and buys that pearl. (Matthew 13:45)(TEV)

> Do not be afraid, little flock, for your Father is pleased to give you the Kingdom. Sell all your belongings and give the money to the poor. Provide for yourselves pursed that don't wear out, and save your riches in heaven, where they will never decrease, because no thief can get to them, and no moth can destroy them. For your heart will always be where your riches are. (Luke 12:32-34)(TEV)

It is apparent that Jesus considered the value of living in the spiritual universe to be greater than any treasure on earth, even life itself. Paul agreed when he said:

> Yet whatever gains I had, these I have come to regard as loss because of Christ. More than that, I regard everything as loss because of the surpassing value of knowing Christ Jesus my Lord. For his sake I have suffered the loss of all things, and I regard them as rubbish, in order that I may gain Christ. (Philippians 3:7-8)(NRSV)

Before we go further in understanding just what being a "child of God" means, we must understand what it does not mean. The ancient Gnostics said that the flesh was evil and only the spirit good, and that the two were separate things. I do not intend to resurrect that old heresy. Becoming a child of God does not relegate the animal body to worthless evil baggage or a curse that we must carry. Instead, God sanctified the human body by having his Son live in one. The body thus becomes the temple of God on earth, his hands and feet, sanctified and honored as the temporal home for the spirit.

> You know that your bodies are parts of the body of Christ. (1 Corinthians 6:15*a*)(TEV)

> I appeal to you therefore, brothers and sisters, by the mercies of God, to present your bodies as a living sacrifice, holy and acceptable to God, which is your spiritual worship. (Romans 12:1)(NRSV)

Paul suggests that even the spiritual universe must have bodies suited to its medium of existence:

> What is sown is perishable, what is raised is imperishable. It is sown in dishonor, it is raised in glory. It is sown in weakness, it is raised in power. It is sown a physical body, it is raised a spiritual body. If there is a physical body, there is also a spiritual body. (1 Corinthians 15:42*b*-44)(NRSV)

A child of God is not better than his fellow humans—set apart, removed. Since it is within their nature, everyone, because of their God-given soul, is capable of becoming a child of God. None can be treated as less worthy and less loved by God. For as long as children of God live on the earth, they have the potential for sin, and thus as long as we are in our animal bodies, we are still one with our fellow human beings.

> Since all have sinned and fall short of the glory of God. (Romans 3:23)(NRSV)

Much modern theology, adopting our cultural humanism, sometimes extols our efforts to become "fully human." We must not be trapped into believing that the moral humanist, the upstanding good citizen, the ideal, successful human being, is necessarily a child of God. So smart are we as intelligent animals that we can see that living by standards of morality and decency (many of them derived from Christ's teachings) ensures a peaceful and respected life. Treating one's fellow humans with kindness is a downright humane thing to do. We even try to treat our fellow animals "humanely."

This, however, does not seem to be the message of the Gospel. The good news that Jesus brought us is to become fully spiritual not fully human. We must have a word of caution here again. As human animals we cannot deny our humanity and all of the functions it entails. To do so is courting destruction, both mentally and physically. But the challenge of the Gospel is to grow into a spiritual creature that lives beyond this existence and not remain forever trapped and controlled by our animal bodies. We must become "more than human." Paul continues:

> But you do not live as your human nature tells you to; instead, you live as the Spirit tells you to—if, in fact, God's Spirit lives in you. Whoever does not have the Spirit of Christ does not belong to him. But if Christ lives in you, the Spirit is life for you because you have been put right with God, even though your bodies are going to die because of sin. If the Spirit of God, who raised Jesus from death, lives in you, then he who raised Christ from death will also give life to your mortal bodies by the presence of his Spirit in you.
>
> So then, my brothers [and sisters], we have an obligation, but it is not to live as our human nature wants to. For if you live according to your human nature, you are going to die; but if by the Spirit you put to death your sinful actions, you will live. Those who are led by God's Spirit are God's sons [children]. For the Spirit that God has given you does not make you slaves and cause you to be afraid; instead the

> Spirit makes you God's children, and by the Spirit's power
> we cry out to God, "Father! My Father!" God's Spirit joins
> himself to our spirits to declare that we are God's children.
> Since we are his children, we will possess the blessing he
> keeps for his people, and we will also possess with Christ
> what God has kept for him; for if we share Christ's suffering,
> we will also share his glory. (Romans 8:9-17)(TEV)

We can become more than just human. We can become children
of God. Perhaps, this is how man is to continue evolution, to evolve
into a creature of the spiritual universe. Perhaps, this is how man is
to go beyond evolution, by becoming a child of God.

So what difference does it make to be a child of God? The
Sermon on the Mount in Matthew 5-7 is a good description, and
Romans 12-15 and Ephesians 4-6 are further expositions that are
worth reading or re-reading.

> You have heard that it was said, "You shall love your neighbor
> and hate your enemy." But I say to you, Love your enemies
> and pray for those who persecute you, so that you may be
> children of your Father in heaven; . . . For if you love those
> who love you, what reward do you have? . . . And if you
> greet only your brothers and sisters, what more are you
> doing than others? . . . Be perfect, therefore, as your heavenly
> Father is perfect. (Matthew 5:43-48)(NRSV)

> He said to him, "You shall love the Lord your God with all
> your heart, and with all your soul, and with all your mind.
> This is the greatest and first commandment. And a second is
> like it, 'You shall love your neighbor as yourself.' On these
> two commandments hang all the law and the prophets."
> (Matthew 22:37-39)(NRSV)

> Let love be genuine; hate what is evil, hold fast to what is
> good; love one another with mutual affection; outdo one
> another in showing honor. Do not lag in zeal, be ardent in

> Spirit, serve the Lord. Rejoice in hope, be patient in suffering,
> persevere in prayer. Contribute to the needs of the saints,
> extend hospitality to strangers. (Romans 12:9-13)(NRSV)

> Therefore be imitators of God, as beloved children, and live in
> love, as Christ loved us and gave himself up for us, a fragrant
> offering and sacrifice to God. (Ephesians 5:1-2)(NRSV)

Basically, children of God love. They love their God and their
neighbor unconditionally. They pray for their enemies, they go
the extra mile, they are not proud or boastful. They bear no grudges
and do not hate their fellow humans. They love and they serve.

> "Lord, when was it that we saw you hungry and gave you
> food, or thirsty and give you something to drink? And when
> was it that we saw you a stranger and welcomed you, or
> naked and gave you clothing? And when was it that we saw
> you sick or in prison and visited you?" And the king will
> answer them, "Truly, I tell you, just as you did it to one of
> the least of these who are members of my family, you did it
> to me." (Matthew 25:37*b*-40)(NRSV)

Becoming God's Child

We recognize this as the Gospel of Jesus Christ who seeks today
to help make us all citizens of the spiritual universe. This is God's
design for us. If, dear reader, you are not a child of God and you
wish to become one, there is nothing more to do than recognize
your willful preference for following your animal instincts and
desires and accept God's forgiveness for this, your sin. Know by
faith that the death of Jesus on the cross represents God's unlimited
love for you as his child, a love so great that it would let his own
Son be sacrificed to all the sin and animal passion of this world,
once and for all time conquering them.

Recognize by faith that the resurrection of Jesus from the dead,
transformed into a spiritual universe body and witnessed by

hundreds of people, is sufficient proof of Jesus' authority and of the existence and ultimate power of the spiritual universe. We will talk about the resurrection in chapter 8. But hear now Paul's witness to the resurrection.

> I passed on to you what I received, which is of the greatest importance: That Christ died for our sins, as is written in the Scriptures; that he was buried and that he was raised to life three days later, as written in the Scriptures; that he appeared to Peter and then to all twelve apostles. Then he appeared to more than five hundred of his followers at once, most of whom are still alive, although some have died. Then he appeared to James, and afterward to all the apostles.
>
> Last of all he appeared also to me—even though I am like someone whose birth was abnormal. For I am the least of all the apostles—I do not even deserve to be called an apostle, because I persecuted God's church. (1 Corinthians 15:3-9)(TEV)

Understand with faith that Jesus Christ is God's still living Son and your ever-present friend; your guide to living victoriously in this world and to entering the spiritual universe. You can communicate with him through prayer and meditation and study.

Undergo a baptism with water to symbolize your birth as a child of God and a citizen of the spiritual universe. As a gift, God will give you his living Holy Spirit, the still living Christ, to be with you, guiding you.

Study the Bible which once was boring but now opens as a beautiful flower of truth because you are reading it with the eyes of faith and with your soul. This, perhaps, is the most common evidence of the guiding presence of the Holy Spirit.

Seek to serve your fellow man as your thanks to God for his life-transforming gift of grace and as your route to spiritual maturity.

Most importantly, join with a group of other Christians for support and encouragement, and the Spirit of God will then guide you as you seek to follow the example of Jesus. Your goal together in life is to become more holy, a task that literally takes forever. You will then be able to live the life abundant with joy, freed of slavery to our animal nature, and anticipating the future freedom of life fully in God's universe.

Remember, Jesus came for all people. It is God's universal religion. If we Western people have made it into culture-justifying religion, that is our sin. Jesus revealed a God urgently seeking to restore all men to a relationship with him. God has acted in history to reunite all his creatures to their rightful place as his children, by giving them full citizenship in both the physical and the spiritual universes.

Can't we just try to live by Jesus' teachings on our own? Why do we have to get involved with all the rituals and rules associated with the church? My only answer is that you can try, as many people have through the centuries, but it is all a trap that our human brains lead us into. If you want to be a part of the spiritual universe, it is best to go by the rules of the spiritual universe and with its earthly institutions that have stood the test of time and faith for thousands of years. The church was instituted by Jesus as his physical body on earth, but like all institutions that involve people, churches have their faults. In fact, they often call themselves hospitals for sinners. But just as the Bible suddenly appears exciting when you accept Christ into your life, so too will the church. They come in all styles and sizes; find one that loves God with a mind open to the truth.

I have tried to word the truth of the Christian faith in terms of the spiritual universe that we have talked about. Remember that this is the most important thing that you can do in your life, not something to be taken lightly. To live in the spiritual universe is to live in the ultimate reality and power of our multidimensional existence in which the physical universe may be only a minor portion.

We begin to live in the spiritual universe immediately ("The Kingdom of God is within you" [Luke 17:21b][TEV]), but we must continue to grow in that realm in the same way that we grow and mature as animals. The analogy is the same. Modern science and the theory of evolution have helped us see our true nature as intelligent animals. The Gospel of Jesus Christ has given us a new understanding of what our nature can be. God seeks to have us all become his children. Physical evolution may work its will on the human body, perfecting it for the earthly environment, but it is spiritual evolution that will help us to evolve into children of God, perfecting us to live in the spiritual universe.

CHAPTER SIX

THE GOD OF CHANCE

God moves in a mysterious way
His wonders to perform;
He plants his footsteps in the sea,
And rides upon the storm.
Deep in unfathomable mines
Of never failing skill
He treasures up his bright designs
And works his sovereign will.
William Cowper

Again I saw that under the sun the race is not to the swift, nor
the battle to the strong, nor bread to the wise, nor riches to the
intelligent, nor favor to the skillful; but time and chance happen
to them all.
(Ecclesiastes 9:11)(NRSV)

Nature is the art of God.
Dante

Jesus taught that God is deeply concerned about us and our
welfare, and that he is actively involved in human history. In
addition, the Gospels tell us that Jesus performed countless miracles
during his life, and Christians since then have been witness to
millions more. Yet science interpreted the world as strictly a cause-
and-effect place with no place for supernatural miracles. Formerly
mysterious forces such as volcanoes, earthquakes, thunderstorms,

and whirlwinds, sickness and health were studied by scientists and identified as mere natural laws at work. The role of God in the world was steadily reduced and science and religion quickly came into conflict.

It wasn't until only recently that science has found the universe cannot be explained entirely by cause-and-effect relationships. Particularly, in the realm of atoms and subatomic particles where forces described by *quantum mechanics* rule, events occur that have no cause. *(We will discuss quantum mechanics more thoroughly in chapter 9.)* Also, very complex systems as diverse as the weather and the stock market respond to the subtlest of forces that are unpredictable in the normal way.

Nevertheless, without a consistency in the cause and effect in most of the universe, science would be hopelessly frustrated in making any sense at all about what it observes. If most events happened without any physical reason, there would be no way to make rational judgments and deductions about anything. We could not even function on a day-to-day basis. So to have science that can improve our stewardship of the earth, we must have consistency. There must be no little miracles popping up here and there to confuse things. Logic must reign. And indeed it does in most events.

It is by the great providence of God that this is so. It may be that in every moment, God is maintaining this consistency by his dynamic will. It is by God's providence that we can even live on this planet and that we can have a means to learn about it—science.

Many people believe that whenever something happens that saves their hide, God's providence—a miracle—has saved them. Someone once described how he had thanked God for saving him when his car had gone off the road. But it was correctly pointed out that it is more in God's providence that, on every other day, his car has been kept on the road. Every moment, God maintains the force of gravity and the laws of physics so our cars will run and their wheels will stick to the pavement. If our cars wreck due to bad construction, our poor maintenance, or our poor driving skills, is it required of God that he rescue us from our mistakes? I would prefer that he keep the laws of nature running smoothly.

Consider the lucky people who had to change a plane reservation and missed a flight that crashed. Were they better Christians and, therefore, more deserving of a miracle than the ones that died? Or were the victims worse sinners and, therefore, being punished for their sins? This is just a restating of that old philosophy that survivors of natural disasters are somehow more righteous or better loved than the victims. In essence, it is blaming the victim. As we saw before, Jesus squelched that idea in his discussion of a terrible murder that had all Galilee buzzing. As Luke described it,

> At that very time there were some present who told him of the Galileans whose blood Pilate had mingled with their sacrifices. He asked them, "Do you think that because these Galileans suffered in this way they were worse sinners than all the other Galileans? No, I tell you; but unless you repent, you will all perish as they did. Or those eighteen who were killed when the tower of Siloam fell on them—do you think that they were worse offenders than all the others living in Jerusalem? No, I tell you, but unless you repent, you will all perish." (Luke 13:1-5)(NRSV)

In addition, Jesus said,

> For he makes his sun to shine on bad and good people alike, and gives rain to those who do good and those who do evil. (Matthew 5:45)(TEV)

God's providence is not determined by how good we are. It is constant and dependable for all his creatures. And it is precisely that which makes science possible. Einstein, who had a hard time accepting the uncertainties of quantum mechanics, insisted that God doesn't play dice.

If God's providence is to maintain the natural laws of the world, how can we say that he also involves himself closely with his creation? Did he start the big bang and then just sit back and wait to see what would happen? That doesn't seem consistent with a loving Father, although so beautiful was his original design, it is possible. I think Jesus was right when he said that God knows everything that happens, even when a sparrow falls or we lose a hair from our heads (Matthew 10:29-31). The example was, possibly, one of the many points he made in exaggeration, but Jesus knew that God was and is involved in the world. How then can we resolve this conflict between science which sees no supernatural action on creation or in anything that occurs, and Christianity that sees God involved in and aware of everything? The answer may lie in the laws of chance.

Taking a Chance

Does everything that happens in the world have a cause? On the level of existence in which we live—yes. But much of what happens in the world has so many interrelating causes and effects that no single causative event can be detected. This is especially so in extremely complex systems, such as biological organisms, where the effects are the result of so many myriad of causes we must often invoke the laws of chance that any single result will happen. The simple tossing of a coin is actually a complex event. The result is determined by the force of the toss, air currents, perhaps, the slight variations in the flexing of the muscles of the hand—a multitude of causes, which give a variability to the outcome that fits the laws of chance. The laws of chance are the estimates of the probability that any one result will occur out of many possible results. These laws are mathematically understandable, and they apply in an enormous number of events that occur in our daily lives

It is the laws of chance that tell us whether the rain will fall (likely if there is a rain cloud overhead), if you will get home without an auto accident (unlikely if there is a lot of traffic and you are a poor driver), if a mosquito will bite you (likely if they are numerous and hungry), and on and on. Some events are so likely to happen that we don't even see the chance in them. These are the direct cause and effects that we see (if the rain falls on you, you will get wet). And some events are so unlikely that we don't even consider them a possibility (the sky will turn green). Yet it can be reasoned that within every possibility there is the chance, albeit sometimes extremely small, that the event will or will not occur.

Some events, such as the disintegration of a proton in the nucleus of the atom, have so small a probability that they may not have happened in the history of the universe. Still scientists reason that there are so many protons in the universe, a proton disintegration should be detected over a reasonably short time scale, even though the probability that any one proton will disintegrate is extremely small. This is one way to change the odds than an event will occur: increase the number of chances for an event to happen. The increased number needed is inversely proportional to the probability. That is, low probabilities need large numbers of events.

It is here in the realm of chance events that God can act. God is the God of chance, because he can influence events by altering the odds—he can cause the unlikely to happen. And is so doing he is totally undetectable by scientific study. This invisible influence is necessary in order that scientific study be even possible. It has been said that we have neglected the fundamental fact that nature is a controlled by both laws of cause-and-effect and laws of chance. For religious people, the random events or chance events in human history are the events of God. And this is the only way in our Judeo-Christian experience that God can act unseen and without direct intervention. As the psalmist said,

> Your way was through the sea, your path, through the mighty waters; yet your footprints were unseen. (Psalm 77:19)(NRSV)

In fact, God acting through chance is biblical. In the Old Testament, the priest used *Urim and Thummim* as some sort of divining devices.

> The Governor told them that they were not to partake of the most holy food, until there should be a priest to consult Urim and Thummin. (Ezra 2:63) (NRSV)

In the New Testament, the disciples cast lots to determine the replacement for Judas as one of the twelve.

> And they cast lots for them, and the lot fell on Matthias; and he was added to the eleven apostles. (Acts 1:26) (NRSV)

One way that God operates within the laws of chance is by greatly increasing the opportunities for an event to occur. Consider the creation of the earth. We know of only one planet with just the right characteristics to make life possible. That doesn't mean others don't exist, but we know that only one in nine are the odds of it happening in our solar system. Assuming quiet systems like ours are required, the possibility for these may be pretty low in our galaxy. A giant star had to be formed and it had to explode and form all of our elements. Then something had to trigger a tiny part of the gases and dust of that star to reform a smaller star and its circling planets. This may be a chance event with low probability. The star must have a planet orbiting in the liquid water zone, and life must form in just the right mix of chemicals. If the odds against any one of these happening isn't great enough, consider what the odds of two happening in sequence are when multiplied together. When we consider the odds of all the things that happened, the odds against it are astronomically large. Yet it did happen once, and perhaps the galaxy is so huge because God needed to increase the probability that it would happen. He probably wanted it to happen many times and so he needed an enormous universe.

Somewhat the same situation applies to evolution. Here God used the enormous periods of time to increase his probabilities. Evolution required millions of years to move past the stage of bacteria. But God is not to be hurried. Everything occurs in its own time. But once or many times, God could influence the outcome by affecting the laws of chance, in other words, by changing the odds.

Another way that God could act to change the odds is by directly changing the tiniest, most unnoticeable event. Once evolution began to move faster, it appears that direct intervention in the laws of chance might have been necessary. If we assume some creature had developed a particular set of traits necessary for the development of future organisms, humans for instance, it is certain that the creature had to face the vicissitudes of life, particularly the threat of being eaten, for he certainly existed on the menu of some other creature. Before he could pass on his genes to his offspring, he had to survive, and perhaps, by chance he escaped the attack of a *Tyrannosaurus rex*. Was it only chance that caused the Tyrannosaurus to be distracted and miss him with a snap of those nasty, powerful jaws? Was the creature just a bit faster than his predecessors or just a bit smarter so that he would survive by natural selection as evolutionary theory maintains? Or did God intervene by twitching some tiny muscle in such a way that our ancestor escaped? God could easily have intervened, totally undetected, yet the tiniest change could have had enormous consequences.

Many extremely complex events seem to be totally random in their occurrence and are unpredictable. It has recently been shown, however, that even these seemingly chaotic events are ruled by beautiful but extremely complex and never repeating patterns of behavior. Modern science has shown that God has even given an order to chaos. Even the tiniest of actions can have enormous effects on these systems that were not noticeable before. It has been said that the fluttering of a butterfly's wing in Beijing can alter the weather in North America, so sensitive are these chaotic patterns. It is apparent then that God could influence vast systems by the tiniest most undetectable changes. Possibly, intelligence was to have evolved from the dinosaurs, as some have suggested, if they had had enough time. But maybe by chance, they were wiped out completely by some cataclysmic event that was precipitated by the tiniest of events somewhere in the far reaches of the solar system where proto-comets are orbiting the sun. Was it completely by chance or was it influenced by a creator who had another design in mind?

The Miracles of Jesus

A third and, perhaps, the most important way that God can act to influence his creation is through our minds. This is especially so, now that he has an intelligent creature to work with. To understand this further, we have to look at the miracles of Jesus. There were two kinds of miracles that Jesus performed, nonhuman and human.

The nonhuman miracles are those such as turning water into wine, walking on water, calming the storm, and feeding the 5,000. These are remarkably unspectacular in the New Testament, and Jesus didn't want to make much of them except to make a point to a few people about who he was. Indeed, his temptation in the wilderness seems to represent his struggle against using his powers to gain followers by doing spectacular demonstrations. We will deal with these again in chapter 9.

The majority of his miracles, however, were human miracles of healing, resurrection, and conversion. Our soul is the spiritual-realm awareness of our minds, and I am certain that God can influence both the health of our bodies and of our minds by healing us through our souls. Again this is undetectable by scientific analysis, just as that part of our existence is not detectable by scientific study. That doesn't make it nonexistent or without influence. Indeed, the spirit level of our minds may be one of the more powerful influences our bodies have. Most doctors will admit they have little hope of curing patients if the patient loses hope or has no desire to live. A positive attitude or even trust in God will not guarantee recovery (nor will a doctor's intelligence or science for that matter), but it has been shown repeatedly to be a big factor in speedy healing.

The evidence is strong that God will only heal those diseases that can be influenced by our minds, because there are some disorders, such as advanced cancer, that God cannot touch by intervention through the mind. I have seen too many people of deep faith pray unsuccessfully for the healing of these types of patients to not think that God might be self-limited in this way. Kushner could come to no other conclusion upon the death of his young son.

> I recognize His limitations. He is limited in what he can do
> by laws of nature and by the evolution of human nature
> and human moral freedom.

Miracles other than healings seem to occur by God influencing our minds. Dave, a friend of mine, and his wife had been praying for God to lead them to witness to a relative living in another state, and as a matter of faith, they decided that if God somehow provided the airplane fare, one of them would go. Dave, from Indianapolis, went to a ball game in Cincinnati one Saturday soon afterward. This led to a fascinating chain of events. A few weeks later a postman came to their door with a letter. It wasn't a special delivery letter, and the man from the post office couldn't explain why he was delivering it, but there he was and there was the letter. The letter was from a man living in Cincinnati. He too had been to the ball game that Dave had attended, and while in the restroom, he had found a slip of paper on the floor with Dave's name and address on it. He would have passed it by, but that name was familiar. It was the same name that was in the wallet he had stolen from a room in the YMCA in Indianapolis during WWII. For some reason he had kept a picture with the name on it all these years and when they matched, he could do nothing else but send Dave the money, some $200 that he had taken thirty years earlier. What are the odds against this series of events all happening at once? Enormously large. Yet many of us can see many seemingly meaningless chains of events leading to unexpected results.

The mind is certainly God's most facile route to reach humans. Dave's story can only be explained by God's influencing the minds of the participants to do the things they did, things that didn't make much sense in themselves. If God wants a mountain moved, he will influence someone to want to move it, and with bulldozer and dynamite, the mountain will be moved.

How else, but through our minds, are people inspired to the greatness of courage and spirit or even of intellect and discovery that we have seen throughout history? (The formation of the Christian church is a prime example ascribed to God.) What is the biochemical basis for this? What molecules are the basis for love and faith and courage? How can such things, so ultimately important to our survival as a living creature, be defined in terms of the physical world? Perhaps, just as the TV set is able to detect electronic signals and turn them into a picture, our minds are receivers of the spiritual nature of God, and they translate the message into thoughts of faith, courage, and love. The brain then converts these thoughts into the actions of our bodies.

Jesus knew that to have people in tune with God, he had to first have their minds. As Christians we know this mind contact as a gift of God—a special gift that comes only to human animals. And when we are reborn as spiritual beings, our spiritual nature becomes an open conduit for the leading of God in our minds.

The rationalist will say there is no proof of God here, no way to test it. And that is the whole point. We can't prove miracles by science because we can't prove God by science. As Paul pointed out in his first letter to the Corinthians,

> For God in his wisdom made it impossible for people to know him by means of their own wisdom. (1 Corinthians 1:21)(TEV)

Is there then any way that we can detect God working? Our rational minds would like evidence just like the Pharisees did of Jesus. The best and only evidence for God is just what it has always been, the final result. Even when God is found to have influenced your life, you cannot detect his action except by observing the final result. You can't see God acting; you can only see the result of his action. You could not see the forces working that raised the mountain or broke down the Berlin wall, but you know that they were acting because you now experience the mountain and the wall is gone. Leslie Weatherhead wrote,

> It is only as I looked *back* that I felt there was a "Hand that guided and a Heart that planned."

Dave didn't realize God was working while he was at the ball game. It was only after that remarkable series of events that he could see the hand of God. It is similar to the lamplighter who used to light the streetlights each night. As the lamplighter moved down the street and twilight deepened, the lamplighter soon could not be seen. Only the result of his labors was visible as the tiny glimmers of light extended farther and farther into the darkness. This is all the proof we have. It is all the proof we will get. Faith supplies the certainty, for faith is the only means of knowing the spiritual level of life.

> To have faith is to sure of the things we hope for, to be certain of the things we cannot see. (Hebrews 11:1)(TEV)

Science and Chance

We have shown how God can involve himself by influencing chance events in life and not be detectable by science. All of our existence is a miracle, in a sense, since God's hand was involved, though unseen. Even science must admit the hand of chance occurrences. Why do many important discoveries seem to happen to just the right person at the right time, by only chance events? Serendipity, the accidental discovery of just the right thing, has been seen very often in science. Perhaps the most interesting accident was the discovery of penicillin by Alexander Fleming. He had been looking for chemicals to kill bacteria and one of his cultures had accidentally been contaminated with a mold from the open window while he was on a vacation. He had left the sample in the sink instead of disposing of it. When he returned, he noticed that the bacteria around the mold growth had died, leaving a clear ring on the agar, and it was thus that he discovered penicillin. Mary Batton tells in *Discovery by Chance, Science and the Unexpected*, that Fleming was amazed that of the thousands of molds, the one producing penicillin had landed on his staphylococcus culture by chance, and that it happened in his laboratory where he was prepared to notice it.

To complete the penicillin story, it must be added that when an attempt was made to rediscover penicillin, Fleming never succeeded, probably because the molds that form penicillin were very rare and required special conditions. Later when the discovery was eventually repeated, a massive effort was mounted to produce enough penicillin for use during WWII. They soon found that the initially discovered strains of mold were inadequate. It was on a cantaloupe in a fruit market in Peoria that a *Penicillium* strain was discovered, which allowed large-scale production of this vital antibiotic.

This doesn't mean that science is all just chance discovery. Rather it is a lot of hard, often tedious, work that produces the new knowledge that we have today. But when the time was right, God acted as he has throughout history. The need was there (World

War II was coming), the level of knowledge had been reached (how to grow bacteria cultures, etc.), the man with the right frame of mind had been trained (Fleming was looking for chemicals that would kill bacteria), and God acted to give us the discoveries that we needed and were advanced enough to be able to use.

Coincidences

Before we leave this discussion of the God of chance, we must talk about coincidences. It is often the strange combination of coincidences that we consider to be miracles. Certainly Dave's story of many connected coincidences points to the strongest evidence of God's hand in the events. Why did the postman deliver the letter personally, even though it was not special delivery? Why did Dave and the thief both go the same ball game? Why did Dave take out the identifying piece of paper? Why did it fall where it could be seen? Why did the thief happen to see it and why did he pick it up? Why had he kept a remembrance of his crime all those years? Each of those events in themselves is unremarkable, but there are just too many coincidences all connected here to be just happenstance.

Still, we must remember that there are coincidences or accidental occurrences that are totally accidental occurrences— they just happen. We once lived on a street called Dayton Drive in Carmel, Indiana. I didn't particularly like the name. Too mundane. Why not something like Eden Glen or Heavenly Lane. Why couldn't our street be named after a tree like all the other streets in our subdivision: Hawthorne, Spruce, Tulip Popular, Ironwood, or Red Oak, for instance? It turns out that our street was named after the developer's grandson Dayton. But the coincidence here for us is that our first apartment was on West Dayton Street in Madison, Wisconsin, and my wife's parents lived across town on East Dayton Street. In addition, my genealogist wife has discovered that her great-grandfather lived on Dayton Street in Sharon, Pennsylvania. Strange coincidences, but probably not arranged by God, unless he had nothing better to do and wanted to manipulate our life in that way. Maybe he arranged it so I could use it as this example of random chance. Of course, then I couldn't use it as an example of random chance.

There are other coincidences that seem to have more meaning in our lives than that Dayton Street followed us. Those coincidences, such as David experienced, and many others that Christians experience when they pray for help and guidance, are very hard to explain except as "God-incidences." It is well established in the Christian experience that as one develops a closer and closer relationship to God, more and more of these things seem to occur. Leslie Weatherhead quoted William Temple who said,

> When I say my prayers I find that coincidences begin to happen.

We don't know the answer, we only know that some coincidences seem to be of God and some of these situations must be mere accidents. My simple rule of thumb is to believe that if it relates to something I have prayed about, it may well be that God was involved, since I have no way to prove it or not. However, since simple accidents are probably the case most of the time, we must realize that coincidences cannot be considered a proof of God. I think, without a doubt, every religion, from worship of rocks, trees, and volcanoes to today's sophisticated monotheism, began by claiming coincidences as proof of God. Certainly, when one virgin thrown into the mouth of a volcano coincided with the cessation of the eruption, more innocents were doomed to be lost when the volcano erupted again. Jesus fought this problem when people tried continually to get him to prove himself by signs and miracles. He said,

> An evil and adulterous generation asks for a sign; but no sign will be given to it except the sign of the prophet Jonah [someone should rise from the dead after three days]. (Matthew 12:39)(NRSV)

We love God, not because we can prove that he exists or because he does little miracles for us. We love God because he loves us and has given us his son whose death and resurrection have provided a means of reconciliation between our Creator and his intelligent animal creation. Our restoration is not left to chance but has been achieved for us by God through Jesus.

The Creator God of both the physical and spiritual universes is the God of all that exists and of all that happens. Most events he must let happen by the laws of the physical universe, but sometimes, probably only rarely in the natural world, he chooses, in his loving wisdom, to act. A nip here, a tuck there, to reach his ultimate will. Maybe it didn't make any difference to God whether the intelligent creature was a descendant of dinosaurs or mammals, but the appearance of an intelligent creature is the evidence of his working. The evidence for God is in the entirety of creation. As we have seen in Romans,

> Ever since the creation of the world his eternal power and divine nature, invisible though they are, have been understood and seen through the things he has made. (Romans 1: 20)(NRSV)

The laws of chance are his vehicle to influence the physical world—but even more so today, our minds are his means to influence mankind.

CHAPTER SEVEN

SCIENCE, THE BRAIN, AND THE SOUL

Gracious is the Lord, and righteous; our God is merciful.
The Lord protects the simple; when I was brought low, he saved me.
Return, O my soul, to your rest, for the Lord has dealt bountifully
with you.
(Psalms 116:5-7)(NRSV)

It requires a lot of courage, perhaps a better word is stupidity, to tackle a subject such as the "soul." The brain is at least a physical entity that science can study, although we are only at the beginning of understanding how the brain works. But with the soul we have something that is difficult even to define, both logically and theologically. It is not an entity that science can study. You cannot measure the soul, you cannot in any way quantitate it, you cannot even locate the soul in the body. Still everyone thinks they have one. Just what is it anyway? The dictionary defines the soul as the non-physical part of us that consists of our immortal or spiritual essence and which involves our thinking, willing and behavior.

Such a definition essentially precludes a scientific approach. As a result, from a scientific point of view the soul does not exist. It must be a figment of the imagination produced by the firing of certain neuronal synapses in the brain. Yet I would be amazed if any scientists, thinking very deeply about themselves, would be willing to admit that they do not have a soul. In a postscript to an essay in *Natural* History magazine, late professor Stephen Gould of Harvard, a self-proclaimed Jewish agnostic, wrote about this good friend, astronomer Carl Sagan who had recently died. He said that although he and Sagan were doubtful about the existence of souls, he hoped they were wrong for then they could spend eternity wandering the universe in conversation and friendship.

The soul is that most fundamental essence of the self: that which exists beyond the mind and beyond the body. It is our self-consciousness, but it exists beyond consciousness. It is our deepest emotional base, but it exists beyond our emotions. It is our deepest sense of identity, of knowing who we are.

In the Bible the terms *spirit* and *soul* are sometimes used synonymously, and in fact, the dictionary lists "soul" as one of the definitions of spirit. But spirit has a number of other meanings, such as ghost, alcoholic beverage, and frame of mind, and enthusiasm such as a team spirit. There are, however, two places in the New Testament in which there is indicated a difference between "soul" and "spirit."

> Indeed, the word of God is living and active, sharper than any two-edged sword, piercing until it divides soul from spirit, joints from marrow. (Hebrews 4:12)(NRSV)
> May the God of peace himself sanctify you entirely; and may your spirit and soul and body be kept sound and blameless at the coming of our Lord Jesus Christ. (2 Thessalonians 5:23) (NRSV)

These may simple be literary devices, but they give you the sense that the writers considered them to be two separate things. In that case, I would have to define "spirit" as the life force (Webster's definition 1) as inherent in the breath. The word "spirit" comes from the Latin word *spiritus* which means breath as well as soul. Since we are considered to be dead if we no longer breathe, this definition fits the life in our bodies quite apart from the soul. Therefore in the rest of the discussion, we will use the term spirit for life force and soul for the part of us that relates to the spiritual universe.

There is no doubt that as human beings our awareness of our soul resides in the brain. That awareness is a thought process but our soul is not a thought process. Our soul is not a thought. It may be enhanced and strengthened, weakened or destroyed by our thoughts, so it is related to our thoughts, but thoughts are a process of the brain. Thoughts are derived from the complex combination and relationships of neurons firing in the brain. They are a physical-world process. When our brains die, our thoughts stop, but our soul goes on. Yet most would agree that the soul greatly influences our thoughts. A strong soul is the source behind our thoughts of courage, love, strength, determination, creativity, and faith. A weak soul will not be able to have much influence on our human animal minds that think of hatred, cowardice, lust, and revenge. So although it is not of the physical universe, a physical entity, the soul must be that spiritual part of us that interacts with the physical universe.

Understanding the Brain

The brain, our organ of the soul, is literally an ultra-complex computer. And science knows very little about this, the most important organ in our bodies. So sophisticated and complex is this system that even our most powerful computers cannot begin to approximate some of these capabilities of the brain. Even to make us walk, maintaining our balance on two legs and at the same time allowing us to be aware of the world around us, is an ability that astounds computer scientists. Our brains are enormously larger than the brain of a butterfly, yet to duplicate the subtle control the butterfly has of his wings, to search out a flower, land on it, procure nectar, and take off again requires such control that computers could only make a crude simulation. And the monarch butterflies not only do that; they fly all the way to a few specific locations in Mexico at the end of the season to wait out the winter. Those activities are conducted by the tiniest speck of gray matter. A bird's subtle control of its feathers in flight demonstrated by its ability to fly through a complex array of branches and miss them all, landing on a tiny twig, continually amazes me. It is far beyond ability of our best computers.

Without so much as a conscious thought on our part, our brain conducts and monitors much of the business of our bodies, most of its chemistry and most of its motion. The blood absorbs oxygen in the lungs and gives it up to the tissues, the brain all the while directing the breathing and the beating of the heart to make that process work. Only a few of our necessary bodily functions are given to us to control.

Scientists today are at only the earliest stages in understanding how the brain, our main computer, works. By the use of very short-lived radioactively labeled glucose that gives off radioactive particles called positrons, they are able to image the parts of the brain that are activated during various thought processes. Such studies are giving them a better map of where the neuronal patterns are that control or affect such thoughts or operations of the body. But that is about all they know. How the neurons are connected, where they are controlled, how they conduct their business, and how it relates to functions is still only guessed at.

A report by J. Madeleine Nash in *Time Magazine* describes some of the understanding of how the brain is formed in the fetus and how it develops after a child is born. Apparently, the first formed neurons begin pulsing immediately, and this pulsing message directs the formation of some of the earliest, most fundamental neuronal connections in the body. The necessary patterns are laid down, and the brain is awash with nerve cells at birth. The brain may be like a computer, but if it is a computer, this one designs itself by the experiences it receives after birth. The nerve cells are either enhanced or are killed off, connected or disconnected, as is necessary for the brain to become what it is to become. And most of this happens in the first few years of life. The major thought patterns, the language patterns, the behavioral patterns are laid down as the computer brain creates itself. For example, it is at this time that children should be learning language, because the brain is designed to lay down the language patterns. To learn a new language is not impossible for adults, but is a very hard thing to do, as I can attest. But for children, this is their work. Children readily adopt the brain patterns that allow them to eventually speak the language they hear from their caregivers. If their parents are German, they will develop the brain pattern that will make them pronounce *th* as if it were a *t*, and it is very difficult for them to pronounce it as in English. But American or English children develop a pattern that allows them to pronounce it easily. The same applies for the many differences in all languages. The brain has set itself into the patterns that it needs to have.

Neuroscientists have made great strides in understanding the various chemicals that the electrical pulse of a nerve generates at the synapse or junction of one nerve fiber with another. Control of the enzymes with specific drugs that either increase or decrease the concentrations of these chemicals has allowed control over people's pain, their appetites, anxieties, moods, and neuroses. Such knowledge has also been a big help in developing drugs for controlling convulsions which result from rapid uncontrolled firing of neurons. We are also aware of the effect of unhelpful drugs such as alcohol and cocaine and the whole panoply of street drugs that destroy the brain while they insidiously make the user feel as if they are enhancing it. The existence of these chemical effects has tempted scientists to conceive of the brain as totally under chemical control, and that our lives are merely the result of some complex chemical reactions that someday can be completely understood.

But as tempting as that concept is, it is wrong. Science has made some progress in understanding how the brain controls various aspects of our bodily functions, but it is totally in the dark in its understanding of why and how we think what we do. We are much more than the sum of our chemistries. We are much more than the sum of our neuronal firings, our electrical brain waves. We think and we have a soul. Modern computers can calculate numbers at phenomenal rates, far beyond the capabilities of the brain, but they still cannot think. They still cannot create; they definitely cannot love.

A number of scientists are working on the problem of computer intelligence, trying to devise a computer system that can think like a human. I doubt that in my lifetime, such a goal will be realized, at least not anywhere near the capability of the human brain. And even if such a computer could be developed, it would surely be doomed to work entirely by logic. It could probably devise the solutions to complex logical problems, but it could not love. It could not dream. It could not imagine. It could not write poetry. It could not write a symphony or a hymn. (Actually there is a computer program that can compose some reasonable music in the styles of the great composers. But it is not truly creating.) Such things are the result of an input from our soul.

Understanding the Soul

So we have returned to the soul, that undeniable part of us that makes us spiritual and alive. Such a thing cannot be chemical. It cannot be a physical entity because a physical entity would immediately cease to exist upon loss of brain function. And if we have been promised anything by God through the resurrection of Jesus, we have been promised that there is more to life than this physical existence. We have a godlike image within us that is not dependent upon our bodies for its reality. Someone has even suggested there is a "God-gene" present in our DNA that may give us the idea of God. It could also be, instead, what allows us to know of God's presence, our antenna to the spiritual universe. But we cannot know of the soul from science; we must look to the Bible to know the soul.

We find the soul talked about in the Psalms. That is not surprising because the Psalms are poetry, and poetry has its great power and beauty because it often seems to be coming straight from the soul. Some examples are

> Bless the Lord, O my soul, and all that is within me bless his holy name. (Psalm 103:1) (NRSV)

> Return, O my soul, to your rest, for the Lord has dealt bountifully with you. For you have delivered my soul form death, my eyes from tears, my feet from stumbling. (Psalm 116:7-8) (NRSV)

More often in the Psalms, the soul is in perilous condition begging for help:

> My soul is consumed with longing for your ordinances at all times. (Psalm 119:20) (NRSV)

> My soul clings to the dust; revive me according to your word. (Psalm 119:25) (NRSV)

> My soul melts away with sorrow; strengthen me according to your word. (Psalm 119:28) (NRSV)

The soul is that part of us that seeks out God and a relationship with him. Since it is the spiritual part of us, it can relate to God.

> In the path of your judgments, O Lord, we wait for you; your name and your renown are the soul's desire. My soul yearns for you in the night, my spirit within me earnestly seeks you. (Isaiah 26:8-9a)(NRSV)

And it is in the New Testament that we have Jesus's authoritative word about the soul.

> "Which commandment in the first of all?"
> Jesus answered, "The first is, 'Hear, O Israel: the Lord our God, the Lord is one; you shall love the Lord your God with all your heart, and with all your soul, and with all your mind, and with all your strength.' The second is this, 'You shall love your neighbor as yourself.' There is no other commandment greater than these." (Mark 12:28b-31)(NRSV)

The great Old Testament commandments were emphasized by Jesus as the first and foremost of all of God's laws for living in both the physical and the spiritual universe. Our heart, of course, does not mean our physical heart, but rather our emotions. But although it is important to love God with our emotions, the commandment does not stop there. To love God with our mind must certainly mean with all our ability to reason with logic. And we must love God with all our strength, all of our physical body, for it is that body that is useful in doing God's work in the world. This includes the second commandment. For to love our neighbor we must be willing to serve him with our physical means, our strength, both mental and physical. And most importantly, the commandment requires that we love God with the soul, our very being itself, that essential spiritual part of us.

When we die, according to Paul, we must have a new spiritual universe body.

> But someone will ask, "How are the dead raised? With what kind of body do they come?" Fool! What you sow does not come to life unless it dies. And as for what you sow, you do not sow the body that is to be, but a bare seed, perhaps of wheat or some other grain. But God gives it a body as he has chosen, and to each kind of seed its own body . . . . There are both heavenly bodies and earthly bodies, but the glory of heaven is one thing, and the earthly is another. There is the glory of the sun, and another glory of the moon, and another glory of the stars; indeed, star differs from star in glory.
>
> So it is with the resurrection of the dead. What is sown is perishable, what is raised is imperishable. It is sown in dishonor, it is raised in glory. It is sown in weakness, it is raised in power. It is sown a physical body, it is raised a spiritual body. If there is a physical body, there is also a spiritual body . . . . For this perishable body must put on imperishability, and this mortal body must put on immortality. (1 Corinthians 15:35-53) (NRSV)

Apparently, the soul needs a body, whether in this physical universe or in the spiritual universe. We can only imagine what type of body that might be. Such a body is not something that we can even begin to describe or define. In chapters 9 and 10 we will allow ourselves to do some speculation regarding such incomprehensibilities. Right now we should concern ourselves with other matters: the health of the soul in this earthly body.

To lose our bodies, even our minds, is nothing compared to loss of our soul. For to lose our soul is to lose everything. Indeed, it is the soul that is of great concern to Jesus for if we have lost our soul, we have lost that part of us which is of the spiritual universe, made up of the same "substance" that God is made of. Jesus warned,

> Do not fear those who kill the body but cannot kill the soul; rather fear him who can destroy both soul and body in hell. (Matthew 10:28)(NRSV)

And Peter,

> Beloved, I urge you as aliens and exiles to abstain from the desires of the flesh that wage war against the soul. (1 Peter 2:11) (NRSV)

The peril of the soul must ultimately be the desires of the flesh, those passions and desires that do not nurture the soul. Surely drug addiction is one of the most dangerous of soul killers. For whether it is alcohol, cocaine, or heroine, these drugs can so possess the mind and body that the soul will wither. Probably, the most devastating part of these addictions is that eventually the victim loses a sense of his soul. The drug becomes their reason for living, their soul. Yet as terrible and life destroying as drugs are, there is another insidious soul killer: addiction to wealth and possessions. Such an addiction and dependency destroys a soul and the soul never comes to the point of realizing it is dying, because it has a constantly reinforced belief in its great worth. Jesus pointed this out in the parable of the rich man.

> The land of a rich man produced abundantly. And he
> thought to himself, "What should I do, for I have no place
> to store my crops?" Then he said, "I will do this: I will pull
> down my barns and build larger ones, and there I will store
> all my grain and my goods. And I will say to my soul, 'Soul,
> you have ample goods laid up for many years; relax, eat.
> drink, be merry.'" But God said to him, "You fool! This very
> night your life is being demanded of you. And the things
> you have prepared, whose will they be?' So it is with those
> who store up treasures for themselves but are not rich toward
> God." (Luke 12:16-21) (NRSV)

As dangerous as these are, the major soul killer is hate. It
corrupts the soul by directing the mind to everything that is evil
about man. Animals do not hate. They may kill, but they rarely
kill for sport, just for food. They certainly do not hate, for there is
no evil in them. But the mind of man can hate and this is one of
the most destructive passions we have. It seems to corrode the soul
in ways that tarnish it beyond recognition by God. Booker T.
Washington has been reported to have said,

> I will not permit any man to narrow and degrade by soul by
> making me hate him.

Most of the world believes that their hatred will punish its
victim, but what they don't understand is that when they hate,
they are the victim. How much we would prefer it to be the other
way. Unfortunately, for as much as we refuse to believe it, hate
destroys the soul of the hater, not the soul of the person hated.
Jesus knew this and it is this destruction of the soul that drove
Jesus to admonish us to do what is totally contrary to our survival
instincts. We are to love our enemies.

> But I say to you that listen, Love your enemies, do good to
> those who hate you, bless those who curse you, pray for
> those who abuse you. If anyone strikes you on the cheek,

offer the other also; and from anyone who takes away your coat do not withhold even your shirt. Give to everyone who begs from you; and if anyone takes away your goods, do not ask for them again. Do to others as you would have them do to you.

If you love those who love you, what credit is that to you? For even sinners love those who love them. If you do good to those who do good to you, what credit is that to you? For even sinners do the same. If you lend to those from whom you hope to receive, what credit is that to you? Even sinners lend to sinners, to receive as much again. But love your enemies, do good, and lend, expecting nothing in return. Your reward will be great and you will be children of the Most High; for he is kind to the ungrateful and the wicked. Be merciful, just as your Father is merciful. (Luke 6:27-36) (NRSV)

To love those who hate us has no basis in physical-world needs and forces. Much of the world thrives on such hatred and competition. So it is apparent that the great reward we are to receive must not be in this world, but in the spiritual world, in a great strengthening of the soul. To love one's enemies, to lend with no return, to give when something has been taken from us, can only be spiritual world concepts—nurture for the soul.

The soul must grow by being fed with spiritual food and God's spirit. A life of faith will build a soul fitted for its life in the spiritual universe. We need our bodies as long as we live here, but they are, after all, only temporary machines to help us function in the physical world. But if we live wholly directed toward satisfaction of the desires of the body, we live as animals live, destined to die without a soul. There has been a host of witnesses for thousands of years that tell us there is a better way. It does not follow the logic of science. It follows the logic of faith. And when we build our soul, we will have a hope that will sustain us through whatever this world does to us.

Beloved, I pray that all may go well with you and that you
may be in good health, just as it is well with your soul. (3
John 2)(NRSV)

We have this hope, a sure and steadfast anchor of the soul.
(Hebrews 6:19a)(NRSV).

When we have our souls anchored in hope, we have peace. It is
a peace in our soul that survives no matter what is assailing us, no
matter what disease is striking our bodies or our brains, no matter
what happens to our fame and fortune, no matter what happens to
those we love. The Christians of the ages and Christians of today
confirm it over and over again:

And the peace of God, which surpasses all understanding,
will guard your hearts and your minds in Christ Jesus.
(Philippians 4:7)(NRSV)

Such a peace can rest nowhere else but in a nurtured soul,
there guarding our spiritual-world connections. It is the highest
attainment of a human being for it brings us citizenship in the
spiritual universe and is what makes us children of God.

CHAPTER EIGHT

THE REALITY OF JESUS

Therefore God also highly exalted him
and gave him the name
that is above very name,
so that at the name of Jesus
every knee should bend,
in heaven and on earth and under the earth,
and every tongue should confess
that Jesus Christ is Lord,
to the glory of God the Father.
(Philippians 2:9-11)(NRSV)

Who was and is the man Jesus that engendered the beautiful words above? At the least, he was a simple Jewish carpenter living in first-century Palestine, who, at thirty years of age, became an itinerant teacher and prophet, and was subsequently crucified by the Romans at the behest of the Jewish religious hierarchy who felt threatened by his teachings. At the greatest, he was raised from the dead and was the Messiah, the Son of God or God himself. If we want to come to the core of the conflict between science and Christianity, it is Jesus. Jesus is the real challenge to us in this scientific age. Scientists have stumbled over Jesus, more than over any other personage of biblical history, not because of the least description of him but because of the greatest. But then people through the ages have stumbled over Jesus, because as Paul said,

> But we claim Christ crucified, a stumbling block to Jews
> and foolishness to Gentiles, but to those who are called,
> both Jews and Greeks, Christ the power of God and the
> wisdom of God. For God's foolishness is wiser than human
> wisdom, and God's weakness is stronger than human
> strength. (1 Corinthians 1:23-25)(NRSV)

Scientists are just people who happen to love to study facts about the physical world. They have no special rights or privileges. They must face Jesus and make a decision for or against him, like everyone else. To many scientists, Jesus is a stumbling block, because faith in Jesus ultimately requires belief in the supernatural, and as such it goes counter to their training as experimentalists. Of course, all of science is ultimately an act of faith in the existence of the physical universe and its knowability, so scientist cannot make a claim that faith is unknown to them.

Nevertheless, science does begin with facts and evidence. So let us look at the facts and evidence for Jesus. We have discussed a simple faith in Jesus in chapter 5 and we will talk a bit about the resurrection of Jesus in chapter 9, but it is a worthwhile exercise to review the evidence for Jesus in a logical sense. Jesus was a man who lived two thousand years ago, and much of the evidence for Jesus must, therefore, be historical evidence. But can it stand up to the scrutiny of people of the twenty-first century? Who was this simple carpenter who founded a religion that was able to conquer the mighty Roman Empire and has, ever since, transformed the whole of human society?

The Facts of Jesus

A host of books have been written in the past two centuries, trying to disprove Jesus ever existed or that he was not who he said he was. Another host of books has tried to prove the opposite, that he existed and is who he said he was. The first book to do the latter is the New Testament. Many historians have discounted it, because it is a book associated with a religion, and therefore cannot be factual.

But there is a vast difference between the books of New Testament and the early stories in Genesis—the New Testament obviously contains eyewitness accounts. These first four books plus the book of Acts were written with the avowed aim of converting people to a belief in Jesus, by telling of his teachings, the events of his life and death, and the reactions and experiences of his followers. The remaining books were written mainly by the apostle Paul, possibly Peter, and a number of other early Christians as an exposition of the faith, and encouragement and correction of the new Gentile Christians. These books were all written in Greek, to a sophisticated audience in the Roman world. Compared with the controversial early stories of Genesis which have been discussed in the first chapters in this book, the New Testament Jesus stories, commonly known as the Gospels, were written within the lifetimes of the people who knew Jesus. As the eyewitnesses began to die off, the urgency of recording their experiences of Jesus was the stimulus for preserving a coherent written record.

As a result, Jesus is the most well-documented personage in the ancient world. We have more timely writings about him than any other ancient person, but because they have been incorporated in the New Testament and have been declared Holy Scripture by the church, skeptical historians have discounted them. They do not fully satisfy the modern standards of historical accuracy, but no ancient literature does and it does not automatically mean they are falsehoods. Actually, they have great validity as authentic for two reasons: First they were written while many of the eyewitnesses were still alive and could have rejected them as untrue. Second, they were widely accepted in the early church, and it is that continued acceptance that eventually gave them status as scripture. It is inconceivable that this would have been so, if they were not reasonably valid accounts. Although there are some differences in descriptions of some of the events in Jesus' life, the early church saw them as such valuable resources for the growth of the faith that this did not concern them. Such inconsistencies are more a problem for modern scholars who demand scientific-like accuracy, though they can never get it even in modern histories. Ancient historians did not worry about such details. The overall story was of most importance.

Let us look at the major aspects of our knowledge of Jesus.

The Birth of Jesus

He was born. Only the Gospels of Matthew and Luke say anything about his birth, and both ascribe it to an act of God upon an unmarried maiden named Mary who was betrothed but not yet joined with a man named Joseph. This event called the virgin birth has been made an absolutely necessary doctrine of belief by many Christians, but it is not. Obviously two of the Gospel writers, Mark and John, the latter of whom wrote expressly to establish the divinity of Jesus, did not mention it. It is apparent that Paul, whose epistles were the earliest writings in the New Testament, did not know about his unique conception, since he made no mention of it. In fact, in the salutation to the book of Romans, Paul states,

The gospel concerning his Son, who was *descended from David according to the flesh* and was *declared to be Son of God* with power according to the spirit of holiness by resurrection from the dead, Jesus Christ our Lord . . .
(Romans 1:3-4)(NRSV) (*italics mine*)

Paul, assuming that Jesus was born as any person was with a natural father (Joseph) and mother (Mary), understood that Jesus the man had been declared to be the Son of God by the Spirit of God and this was attested to by his resurrection from the dead. So if Paul did not find the virgin birth a necessity of faith, it cannot be so. It may well have happened, but it must never be made a requirement for salvation.

If Jesus were the son of God and not truly Joseph's son, then he would not be a valid descendent of David. The two genealogies of Jesus, one in Matthew and one in Luke, the very Gospels that tell of his virgin birth, both give a genealogy from David through Joseph. So if Jesus was descended from David, he must have been so through Mary. But it is also interesting that Jesus seemed to be refuting the notion that the Messiah must be descended from David when he quoted Psalm 110: 1 to some Sadducees and said,

How can they say that the Messiah is David's son? For David himself says in the book of Psalms,
     "The Lord said to my Lord,
     'Sit at my right hand, until I make your enemies your footstool.'"
David thus calls him Lord; so how can he be his son?
(Luke 20: 41-44)(NRSV)

It is possible that, having been brought up in a small community where everyone may have known that his mother had been pregnant (from God) before her marriage, Jesus possibly wasn't sure he was descended from David. He was sure, however, that he was the Messiah. These very uncertainties help to authenticate the

Gospels, because if they had been a concocted tale, the author would never have allowed such doubt to arise.

So where does this concept of the virgin birth come from? The author of Luke, who wrote the most detailed description of Mary's divine conception, was probably Luke, the physician, a contemporary and companion of Paul (see Colossians 4:14, 2 Timothy 4:11 and Philemon 24). He has been the ascribed author of the Gospel bearing his name and the book of Acts since early times. Luke, although he was not an eyewitness to Jesus' life, declares in the beginning of the Gospel,

> Since many have undertaken to set down an orderly account of the events that have been fulfilled among us, just as they were handed on to us by those who from the beginning were eyewitnesses and servants of the word, I too decided, after investigating everything carefully from the very first, [or for a long time] to write an orderly account for you, most excellent Theophilus, so that you may know the truth concerning the things about which you have been instructed. (Luke 1:1-4)(NRSV)

Apparently accuracy was of special importance to Luke because for him to have his work accepted, it must pass the test of acceptance of the eyewitnesses, some of whom were certainly still alive and were his sources of information. Tradition says that Mary the mother of Jesus lived long enough to pass this birth information on to Luke.

But although the virgin birth challenges our modern sense of natural conception, it becomes validated not by the accounts in the Gospels but by the event that Paul said justified God's bestowal of sonship upon Jesus, *the resurrection.* You may accept the virgin birth by faith or reject it as improbable, but there is this one event in Jesus life that determines and validates all the others, *the resurrection.* Certainly, the early Christians, totally rejuvenated by the witness of the resurrected Christ, sought to understand this God-man who lived among them. Understandably, he had become divine and they needed to find support for this in his origin. Since the resurrection was an established witnessed fact, the virgin birth was a corollary event that fully was supported by his final destiny.

The Resurrection

So we must now go to the real beginning of the story of Jesus, the resurrection. Indeed, the resurrection is not the end of the Jesus story, but the beginning. That we know anything at all about Jesus is because of the resurrection. No Gospels would have been written, no churches formed, no martyrs sacrificed, no conversion of the mighty Roman Empire. There would be no evidence of Jesus at all if it hadn't been for the resurrection. All that Jesus said and did while alive is authenticated and given utmost importance and significance because of the resurrection. His teachings, his miracles are all important because he was raised, and so all of what we know about Jesus ultimately rests on the proof of the resurrection.

A scientist demands evidence that an event really happened as it is reported. Unfortunately, historical events cannot be reenacted and it is necessary to look at eyewitness reports and subsequent events that relate to the incident in question. For the resurrection we have both—eyewitness accounts and historical effects. It is without a doubt the most well-documented event in ancient history and the effects on the history of the world have been enormous.

The first evidence comes from the fact that there are four separate accounts of the resurrection written by four different authors, three who could be eyewitnesses and one who learned of it from talking with eyewitnesses. This would be unthinkable if the resurrection had been dreamed up by the apostle Paul, as some have suggested. An imagined or contrived event would have been allowed only a single author, who would not have tolerated any variation in the account. Consider the Islamic Qur'an, which was reportedly dictated to Mohammed by God, and no commentary or versions in other languages were allowed. Not so the Gospels of the risen Jesus. He was witnessed by so many people that it would have been impossible to dictate a single version. So the four Gospel accounts are one of the strongest indications of the authenticity of the resurrection.

The second evidence is the report of eyewitnesses. Matthew, Mark, and John could well have been eyewitnesses to the resurrected Christ. In addition, Paul speaks of many witnesses still living along with his own belated meeting with Jesus.

> For I handed on to you as of first importance what I in turn had received: that Christ died for our sins in accordance with the scriptures, and that he was buried, and that he was raised on the third day in accordance with the scriptures, *("Scriptures" here are referring to the Old Testament.)* and that he appeared to Cephas [Peter], then to the twelve. Then he appeared to more than five hundred brothers and sisters at one time, most of whom are still alive, though some have died. Then he appeared to James, then to all the apostles. Last of all, as one untimely born, he appeared also to me. (1 Corinthians 15:3-8)(NRSV)

If that many people who had witnessed the resurrected Jesus were still alive, it would be difficult to preach anything else without being quickly refuted. If so many of his followers were still alive, it would have been very difficult to preach a risen Christ if it had not happened.

The third evidence is the cross as a Christian symbol. The crucifixion of Jesus should have been the end of his group and his movement as the execution of the leader has been for hundreds of messianic cults. The Romans knew this, and for this reason, were willing to support the Jewish leadership in removing Jesus from the scene. It would give them one less group of agitators to worry about. But the resurrection changed that. The resurrection kept the group alive and very soon among them, it transformed the cross on which he died from an instrument of terror, torture, and death to a beautiful symbol of God's love for humankind. In the Roman culture, it would take something very powerful to do that.

The fourth evidence comes from the revival of the followers of Jesus into a group that turned the world upside down.

> When they could not find them, they dragged Jason and some believers before the city authorities, shouting, "These people who have been turning the world upside down have come here also." (Acts 17:6)(NRSV)

Totally devastated by the crucifixion of Jesus, his followers were undoubtedly the most demoralized people in the world. Their leader, Peter, had just denied knowing Jesus three times. None of these people were very sophisticated and it would have been out of character for them at this time to fabricate a resurrection tale that they could not even believe themselves when they were first presented with the facts.

> Now it was Mary Magdalene, Joanna, Mary the mother of James, and the other women with them who told this to the apostles. But these words seemed to them an idle tale and they did not believe them. But Peter got up and ran to the tomb; stooping and looking in, he saw the linen cloths by themselves; then he went home, amazed at what had happened. (Luke 24:10-12)(NRSV)

> But Thomas (who was called the Twin), one of the twelve, was not with them when Jesus came. So the other disciples told him, "We have seen the Lord." But he said to them, "Unless I see the mark of the nails in his hands, and put my finger in the mark of the nails and my hand in his side, I will not believe."
> A week later his disciples were again in the house and Thomas was with them. Although the doors were shut, Jesus came and stood among them and said, "Peace be with you." Then he said to Thomas, "Put your finger here and see my hands. Reach out your hand and put it in my side. Do not doubt but believe." Thomas answered him, "My Lord and my God!" (John 20: 24-28)(NRSV)

These same disciples were soon preaching and convincing thousands of people of the resurrection of Jesus. The resurrection was the cornerstone of Peter's and of Paul's preaching. Everything that they said was based on their conviction of a risen Christ. This unshakable conviction was what gave them the power to ultimately conquer the Roman Empire. This conviction gave them the strength to withstand unthinkable persecution and death. It is the same conviction that is the basis for the church today, two thousand years later.

A fifth evidence for the resurrection is that very soon, Christians began to worship on Sunday, the first day of the week, instead of Saturday, the Jewish Sabbath. The biblical basis for Sabbath worship is so strong that it is unthinkable that they would have changed the day of worship unless some very important event had occurred. The rising of Jesus on the first day of the week proved to be the event of such earth-shaking importance that the early church was willing to make the change.

The Logic of God

One of the remarkable things about Jesus is that he taught concepts of God that were totally contrary to the way that the human animal thought. The parables of the Prodigal Son, the Workers in the Vineyard, the Good Samaritan are excellent examples. In addition, he taught that we are to go the second mile, give our coat to one who asks for it, turn the other cheek, and even to love our enemies. Such concepts are so different from the social code developed by humans that they are shocking to us. But these teachings immediately reveal to us that Jesus is using the logic of God, not the logic of human experience and tradition. That deserves a thorough discussion in itself, but the point that I wish to make here is that Jesus, his life, teachings, and death are all part of the logic of God.

Why did Jesus come when he did? Why not earlier, why not later? Probably, there was no better time. Rome controlled most of the known western world. There was good, relatively safe transportation. Writing and literature had firmly taken their place as a means of communication of ideas.

> But when the fullness of time had come, God sent his Son, born of a woman, born under the law. (Galatians 4:4)(NRSV)

Jesus, born of a poor woman and raised like any other poor child, at age thirty, emerged into the society of the common people in an impoverished country in the Roman Empire. He became an itinerant teacher and healer, but his teachings so unnerved the Jewish religious leaders that they sought and succeeded with the help of Rome to have him executed. None of this is the way in which humans would design a Messiah, nor was it the way most of the Jews anticipated him to be. They wanted a conqueror who would throw the Romans out. But Jesus lived by God's logic. That he should then be resurrected from the dead is so inconceivable to man that it has been the principal stumbling block for many people and especially scientists who try to ground themselves in reality. But the logic of the life, death, and resurrection of Jesus is beautiful and profound, even if totally unexpected.

> But as it is written, "What no eye has seen, nor ear heard, nor the human heart conceived, what God has prepared for those who love him." (1 Corinthians 2:9)(NRSV)

There are others in the Bible who are purported to have not died. It is reported in 2 Kings 2 that Elijah was taken up into heaven in a whirlwind and a chariot of fire. But he was not killed. His time was just up. Some Jews also believe that Moses did not die but was taken directly up into heaven. This is not biblical, because Deuteronomy 34:5-8 describes the death of Moses. So, even though such supernatural events were in their beliefs, first-century society did not really conceive of such events very likely. Jesus' raising of Lazarus and a girl who had died brought astonishment but not necessarily belief.

If God wanted to find a way to finally get his message across to humanity, and to show them that he has unlimited love for his creation and also unlimited power over life and death, he could not have chosen a better way. Even though the logic is of God, it is clear enough when we look at it from God's point of view, that even the mind of man can understand it. God wanted a worldwide, timeless religion that would allow people to be restored to a relationship with him. He obviously succeeded, even though the reception is still not unanimous. It probably never will be. But any type of militaristic or humanistic messiah would have long been destroyed and forgotten. It is difficult to imagine any other way that God could have touched humanity with the power that Jesus brings. Obviously, he has reached out to other men such as Siddhartha Gautama (Buddha) and Mohammed, but none can compare with Jesus, whose death and resurrection dramatically demonstrate God's ultimate power. The resurrection of Jesus reveals that God has power over that equalizer of all people, death itself. Humans, through science, have made great strides in preventing untimely death—they have even tragically sometimes delayed its inevitability, but the death rate is still 100 percent. All of us must face it and all of us are impotent to prevent it. Only God in Jesus has demonstrated and declared the victory.

PART II

OUT OF THIS WORLD

Some speculation that the facts of science allow us
to make about God

CHAPTER NINE

WHERE IS GOD?

Where can I go from your Spirit?
Or where can I flee from your presence?
If I ascend to heaven, you are there;
If I make my bed in Sheol, you are there.
If I take the wings of the morning
and settle at the farthest limits of the sea,
even there your hand shall lead me,
and your right hand shall hold me fast.
If I say, "Surely the darkness shall cover me,
and the light around me become night,"
even the darkness is not dark to you,
the night is as bright as the day;
for darkness is as light to you.
(Psalm 139:7-12)(NRSV)

In 1961, when Russian astronaut Yuri Gagarin flew into space, he proclaimed with atheistic delight that he had been to heaven and God wasn't there. Only the most primitive theology was bothered by that fact, however, for today, very few really believe that heaven is up and hell is down. Science has cleared up that ancient misunderstanding long ago. When one lives on a spherical planet, up may be down and down may be up to someone living on the other side. In space, the definition of up and down becomes even more meaningless. Where is God if he isn't up above in heaven?

Jesus said that God was a spirit (John 4:24). But he didn't give a definition of exactly what a spirit is. Clearly Jesus meant a specific entity—not just a state of mind, as we often use the term in English, meaning an attitude, a mind-set, such as a spirit of adventure or love or loyalty. The Spirit-God that Jesus describes is not a concept but an actual reality, a being, a personality. John Robinson, the bishop of Woolwich, in his book *Honest to God*, described God as the "ground of our being." That is certainly one aspect of his multifaceted nature, but it is awfully hard to love the "ground of our being," let alone serve it. Jesus was much more specific about the nature of God's personality. He called God "Father" and when he used the Aramaic word "*Abba*" (Mark 14:36), he was using the familiar sense of "Daddy" that a child uses. Here was no abstract concept, but a warm, loving personality that is most closely imaged in this life by loving human parents.

Human animal minds are limited to human animal concepts and the image of the father is the nearest image to the personality of God that Jesus could find. Today we rightly insist that God is also like a loving mother, but this was too impotent an image for the people of Jesus' day. Only in more recent generations has it been possible in the Protestant church to conceive of the motherly nature of God. The Catholic Church long ago sensed the need for personifying this aspect of God and created the theology of Mary to accomplish it. We must realize that Jesus could only use the father image in his time, for the father was the center of authority and lineage. There were many loving fathers, and Joseph must have been especially loving to Jesus for him to use the name so lovingly for God. But today the image has to include the nature of mother as well. The better term "parent" seems to lack the personal connotation. We will therefore use the traditional term "father."

Unfortunately, all of these are only anthropomorphic or humanlike descriptions of God, and like Michelangelo's portrait of God as a bearded old man, they don't help much in understanding what a spirit is. So what can science do to help us, especially since I have just said that science is limited to discerning the physical universe? Well, frankly, science can't tell us very much. But some interesting developments have taken place recently that may shed some light, at least, on the existence of the spiritual universe itself.

This evidence for the existence of more than just the physical universe came when physicists and mathematicians began to probe the nature of the atom, the smallest unit of any chemical element that exists. It might be useful to digress for a brief review of atomic theory before we try to explain this.

The Atoms of us all

The discovery of radioactivity, which comes from the nucleus of the atom, revealed that atoms consist of two parts: a swirling cloud of negatively charged electrons and a tiny positively charged nucleus, which keeps them in tow. The outer electrons are involved in joining atoms together to make molecules that comprise all substances other than the pure elements themselves. (The science of chemistry works at this level.) The nucleus, though very small (only one-trillionth of the volume of the atom), contains nearly all of the mass (here physics reigns). Please note that only one-trillionth of you is what we define as matter, the rest is empty space. What feels solid or liquid to the touch is not actually the atom center itself, but just the swirling clouds of electrons orbiting the nucleus. When you kiss your spouse, you are really only smooching his or her electron clouds.

The physicists reasoned that if particles were emitted from the nucleus during radioactive decay, the nucleus could not be a homogeneous entity but must consist of different parts. These parts were identified as protons (positively charged) and neutrons (bearing no charge but having equal mass to that of a proton). These particles account for essentially all of the mass of the atom. Each atom has a definite number of protons and therefore an equal number of electrons surrounding the nucleus to make it electrically neutral. It is this number that determines what substance the atom is, sodium, oxygen, iron, gold, or lead, for instance. The neutrons help to determine the total mass of the atom and different numbers of neutrons form what are called isotopes (forms of an element with slightly different atomic weights). Some of these proton-neutron combinations are unstable and spontaneously decompose, giving off the radiation we call radioactivity. Each radioactive isotope decays at a unique rate with a half-life (time it takes for one-half to be gone) that has not changed throughout history and which is one of the reliable constants of the universe.

The physicists probed more deeply into the nucleus using high-energy particle beams and opened a Pandora's box of problems. It wasn't long before they discovered that each proton and each neutron were made up of three subatomic particles called quarks, and these came in three types or "flavors"—up, down, and strange— so that the proton is made up of two up quarks and one down quark while a neutron is made up of two down quarks and one up quark. (Don't let the terminology confuse you. It is just the tongue-in-cheek attempt by physicists to describe characteristics that make no sense at all in our large-scale world.) To make matters worse, they found many more particles which they called such names as mesons, gluons, Z particles, W particles, and neutrinos. Besides these, they found antiparticles of exactly the opposite nature to many of them.

It was also discovered that light, which was always thought to be an energy wave, behaves also like a particle with no mass. The electron, which was thought to be a low-mass particle, was shown to behave like a wave. This led to the concept that the subatomic binding forces were really particles or "quanta" of energy that seemed to pass between the other particles to bind them together. The "quantum theory" was devised to explain all of these strange properties of matter on such a small scale, and this theory has been corroborated again and again by scientific experiment. In addition, Einstein, in his "theory of relativity" had shown how matter and energy were interrelated by his famous equation $E=mc^2$. It is somewhat an understatement to say that modern atomic physics has turned our understanding of the nature of matter upside down.

Science had begun to reach the limits of its ability to even study this subatomic zoo so the mathematicians stepped in to help. In an attempt to make sense of this bewildering array of forces, particles, waves, matter, and energy, a mathematical approach to simplification of all of this was undertaken and is eagerly pursued today. It was Einstein's idea still shared by many in physics, that all matter and energy, and therefore, all of the physical universe itself could be explained by what physicist John Archibald Wheeler calls an "utterly simple idea."

Physicists and mathematicians have made steady progress in combining first the forces of electricity and magnetism and then the weak and strong atomic forces into a mathematical unity. Currently only gravity remains outside their grasp. They are confident, though, that all of the fundamental forces of nature were united as a single force in the enormous temperature and pressures that existed during the first moments of creation of the universe, the "big bang."

These attempts at understanding the fundamental forces of the universe have led to a remarkable discovery. The theoreticians have found that the universe cannot be described mathematically in only three dimensions. The height, weight, and depth measurements that describe all that we know, no longer suffice to fit the universe into a mathematical description. In 1919, Polish physicist Theodor Kaluza proposed a five-dimensional universe, one more than Einstein's three spatial dimensions plus time as a fourth. Kaluza's concept was able to connect Einstein's theory of relativity with Maxwell's electromagnetic equations. But this idea languished when it was shown that electron orbits would be unstable in a space with more than three dimensions. However, a more recent theory called supersymmetry has found that besides the dimension of time that Einstein evoked, seven other dimensions are necessary to explain the interrelationship of matter and energy on a subatomic scale. The theorists took the suggestion of Swedish physicist Oscar Klein and proposed that these extra dimensions are curled up very small, smaller than the nucleus of the atom. The seven dimensions were selected because special mathematical properties are associated with seven dimensional spaces.

The Dimensions of God

Rather than go more deeply into this subject, which is only really understood by the experts in the field, suffice it to say that it is the discovery that the universe consists of more than three dimensions that can bring us back to an understanding of where God is. Way back in the nineteenth century, some people proposed that God was not just three-dimensional but rather four- or more-dimensional and that the spiritual universe could therefore exist. The idea was not been given much respect as modern science began to emerge in the twentieth century, but we could now come around to a reemergence of this concept. Only today has science come to the suggestion that indeed there is more to the universe than three dimensions.

What does it mean to have more than three dimensions? Our minds, which are products of an apparent three-dimensional physical universe, are incapable of thinking of anything more than three, because all of life as we know it can be measured in these three units. We cannot even conceive of where the fourth dimension could go. Yet today computers routinely work in as many dimensions as they wish. Instead of three perpendicular axes of geometry, they use four or five or a thousand. In the simplest mathematical form, this merely involves adding a larger exponent to the equation. For example if x describes a one-dimensional line, the area of a two-dimensional square is defined as x^2 and the volume of a three-dimensional cube is x^3. Although we can't imagine what it would be like, a four-dimensional object is defined as x^4 and a five-dimensional equal-sided object would be x^5 and so on. Computers have drawn three-dimensional images of a four-dimensional hypercube. If you can even begin to understand that, try to imagine a four-dimensional sphere. Only the mathematicians can.

But just because we cannot mentally relate to such a universe in no way means that such a universe does not exist. The fact that it is mathematically possible and the universe is not explained in only three dimensions suggests indeed that our universe may be many-dimensional. If seven other dimensions can be curled up in a tiny space, what is to prevent other dimensions from existing in enormous space? A two-dimensional plane may be wholly contained in a three-dimensional space, and likewise a three- or seven- or eleven-dimensional universe could be wholly contained in a higher-dimensional space.

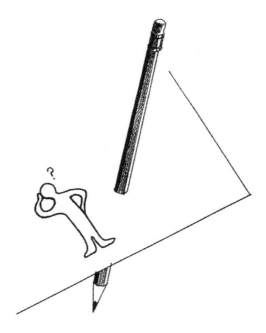

In 1884, Edwin Abbott wrote a book called *Flatland.* In it he proposed a way to gain some understanding of a four-dimensional existence by comparing our three-dimensional space to that experienced by an imaginary two-dimensional creature living in a plane called "Flatland." Mr. Flatlander knows no up or down. He only understands directions in his plane, right or left or forward or back with all the two-dimensional variations in between. An interesting thing occurs when we try to interact with Mr. Flatlander. If we try to poke a sharpened yellow wooden pencil through his world, he sees only a tiny black dot, growing into a black circle which turns into a growing brown circle as the point of the pencil moves past. The brown circle eventually becomes a yellow hexagon remaining for some time. Finally the yellow hexagon becomes a silver circle as the metal eraser holder moves through, and then a pink circle forms, which after a brief appearance disappears altogether as the pencil passes completely through. A three-dimensional pencil has moved through his plane of existence, his two-dimensional world, and he experienced it as circles and hexagons. If we were to put our fingers onto his plane, he would see only five roughly circular different sized spots appear. (If you wonder how a flatlander could determine a circle without viewing it from above, consider how we can determine a tall column is round. We cannot see the other side, but we can determine it is so by moving around the column. So it would be with the Flatlander.)

An interesting characteristic of Flatland is that a three-dimensional being can enter a two-dimensional room without going through any two-dimensional walls. A three-dimensional being can remove things from a two-dimensional safe without even opening the door. He can remove the yolk from a two-dimensional egg without breaking the shell. And he can enter into Mr. Flatlander's heart and mind without cutting through his two-dimensional skin.

This tale can go on and on. I hope that it gives you a feeling for the relationship of dimensions to our understanding of the world. Like Mr. Flatlander, we are mentally trapped in the world of our birth, his two-dimensioned and ours three-dimensioned. He cannot conceive of our three dimensions and we cannot conceive of four. Just consider, before we proceed, that a Flatlander definition of a three-dimensional being might be that he was a ghost, or better yet, a spirit who was not subject to the limitations of the two-dimensional world.

Is the spiritual universe extra-dimensional? We must look to the Bible, our principal source of information on the spiritual universe, to give us clues. And the evidence that we see there is much stronger than that suggested by science. Christianity is founded on the premise that the spiritual universe exists. Indeed, Jesus teaches that the spiritual universe is the primary universe, and it contains the real power.

For mortals it is impossible, but for God all things are possible.
(Matthew 19:26)(NRSV).

His resurrection, (the best documented event in ancient history) in addition to confirming the authenticity of his teaching, shows above all else that the spiritual world is more powerful than death itself, the one event in our lives that reduces all life and human power to a common denominator. (Death is a necessary part of the physical universe because matter and energy must be conserved; resources are limited and must be reused. Only when man developed his self-consciousness and intelligence was there a desire and a God-given means to circumvent death.) Jesus' victory over the ultimate power in the physical world lends credence to his insistence that the spiritual universe is the more important and powerful realm. As the Bible describes it, the spiritual universe is the source of the physical universe. The physical universe may be nothing more than a warp in the dimensions of the spiritual universe, an illusion of reality in a multidimensional universe that is the true reality.

Another way to look at this is that all of existence is within God. He is the basic medium of our reality or as we have said before, "the ground of our being."

For 'In him we live and move and have our being.' (Acts 17:28)(NRSV)

So if this is true, everything that happens, happens in him, inside his multidimensional substance, whatever his substance is. We are a mere extension of that substance. It is certain from past history that God allows us almost total freedom, but we are impotent to move outside of him. Just as all things that exist in the ocean are shaped and controlled by the water they live in, all things that ride on its surface must be shaped and controlled according to the properties of water. The whale and the porpoise were originally land mammals, but to live successfully in the sea they had to evolve to look like fish. All things that fly in the air and all things that walk on the land are in a sense controlled by the medium in which they live. There is freedom to move about and exist independently within that medium, but to challenge the medium itself and try to live without it quickly brings destruction. Just as the astronauts can only live in outer space by bringing our earthly atmosphere with them inside a capsule, shuttle, or space suit, we cannot exist outside of God. For it is within him that we are created and where we live. To do otherwise brings only death.

The evolution of intelligence then has been shaped and molded by the image of God within whom it was formed. It could be nothing else. Life evolved in the medium that is God and his mere presence shaped and molded it just the way it had to be. Perhaps the variety of creatures was allowed some freedom to form, but the final result could only be what God's substance allowed. His multidimensional unseen hand in creation and history is largely, then, the controlling and limiting substance of his very being.

Jesus, the founder of our faith, although fully human, lived as though he was not totally bound by the physical universe in the way we are. He had ready access to the spiritual universe.

> You belong to this world here below, but I come from
> above. You are of this world, I am not of this world.
> (John 8:23)(TEV)

Aside from his healing miracles, some of his actions appear to be very multidimensional. Consider the transfiguration that took place on the mountain and was witnessed by three of his disciples (Luke 9:28-36). He was changed in appearance and was seen to be talking to two other figures identified as Moses and Elijah. Then suddenly they were gone. Consider the other physical miracles such as changing water into wine (John 2:1-11), walking on water (John 6:16-21), and the feeding of the 5,000 (Matthew 14:13-21). The movement of the wine and fish from another dimension into our world would appear quite miraculous, while being rather a mundane thing for a multidimensional person to do. Consider that he sometimes strangely passed through a hostile crowd (Luke

4:30), an easy feat if you use another dimension. But it is the resurrection and the post-resurrection events that give the clearest indication of the multidimensional nature of the risen Christ. He, of course, returned to some form of life after his death and entombment. But although he could eat (John 21:12, Luke 24:43) and be touched (Luke 24:38-40, John 20:27), he could also appear suddenly in a closed room (John 20:19 and 26), or he could disappear before the eyes of the two who were to eat with him in Emmaus (Luke 24:31). These accounts do not appear to be legends, because the writers describe them with the greatest incredulity (Mark 16:8, 11, 13, Luke 24:11, 37, 41, John 20:25). Such events are in no place taken for granted. His followers were as surprised as we are. Finally, he was lifted up and disappeared into heaven (Acts 1:9). Not at all impossible for a man of the other-dimensional spiritual universe, although the word "up" may be a futile attempt to explain a direction of movement that no one can understand.

So where is God? Wherever he is, he is capable of being everywhere in the physical world at once, in, out, up, down, everywhere. One could imagine that he is more than a four-dimensional being. Perhaps he is six- or seven-dimensional. More probably, God is infinitely dimensional—an appealing concept in the light of the new discoveries. This was actually first proposed by the theologian, Arthur Wellink, in 1893. He wrote,

> This emphasizes very strongly what has been said about the Omniscience of God. For he, dwelling in the Highest Space of all, not only has this perfect view of all the constituents of our being, but also is most infinitely near every point and particle of our whole constitution. So that in the most strictly physical sense it is true that in Him we live and move and have our being.

An interesting symbol for God might be derived from this concept of God as infinitely dimensional. As we have shown, an equal-sided four-dimensional object could have its volume or nature described as x^4. Since God is infinite, let us consider that God might be x^∞ (∞ is the mathematical symbol for infinity). And if we change x to X (chi) which is also the first letter of the name of Christ in Greek, we have X^∞ which in mathematical parlance states that God is Christ to the infinite power. And this is exactly what Jesus said he is.

$$God = X^\infty$$

CHAPTER TEN

IS ANYONE ELSE OUT THERE?

In my Father's house there are many dwelling places.
If it were not so, would I have told you that
I go to prepare a place for you?
(John 14:2)(NRSV)

It is still in the realm of total speculation to consider the possibility of other intelligent life in the universe. Actually, the existence of intelligent life here on earth is sometimes in doubt, when we see our fellow man, in all his foolishness, trying to act like God, but really only being an over-smart animal, fighting, cavorting, and despoiling the only home he has. Still, even after some effort to search, there is no indication, whatsoever, that life exists anywhere except here on the silver blue planet, Earth, orbiting the star called Sun in the outskirts of the Milky Way galaxy. When I first wrote those words, that last statement was true, but there have been suggestions based on meteorite fragments that originated on the planet Mars and finally landed in the Antarctic, that bacterial life may have been present on Mars. Although this seems to be unlikely, now, based on the evidence in this meteorite, NASA is still searching for evidence of life on Mars. The significance would be that life may form easily and therefore is very common in the universe.

We have discussed the odds that there are other planets silently circling other stars; planets where life resembling ours can form and flourish. Since planets, such as earth, only shine by reflected light, in other star systems, they would be too dim to be seen by even our most powerful telescopes. Such dim reflections are easily drowned in the brilliance of the parent star. Recently, there has been strong confirmation of the existence of planets in other star systems based on the perturbations of the stars' orbits. Before long, the Hubble space telescope or some ingeniously designed earth-based telescopes may well get the first pictures of another nonsolar planet.

Remember, we said earlier there is only a narrow band of space around any star where liquid water can exist, an almost certain prerequisite for life. Life needs water-soluble carbon chemistry. Since elements are the same universally, it is hard to conceive of life using any other elemental system other than carbon based. None of the other elements have the properties required. Some scientists have suggested that life could be based on ammonia, silicon, or other elemental systems, but it is extremely doubtful. Only carbon/water has the chemical properties to produce the complex molecules of sophisticated life-forms and the complexity required for intelligence. Unless, of course, the original carbon-based life has been robotized. Chemistry is chemistry, and astronomical evidence and the big bang theory indicate that, indeed, chemistry is the same all over the universe. Different pressures and temperatures might allow other chemical systems to become organized, but that is only speculation. We know that carbon/water chemistry works and works well, under a vast range of environments from near 200°C to well below freezing, from near vacuums to the high pressure of the ocean. No doubt, the Creator designed it that way.

So if other planets are going to have a chance for life similar to ours, they are going to need a carbon/water system. It has happened once in the history of the universe. Has it happened elsewhere, now or in the past? In chapter 6 we discussed the chances for this to occur along with the possibility that God increases his chances for living planets to happen by making the universe so immense. If he needed only one living planet, why did he make such an enormous universe? Surely he could have arranged the odds so that only a single solar system was needed—or maybe only a single tiny galaxy. But did he really need billions of stars in a galaxy and billions of galaxies just to get one small planet suitable for life? There is no doubt that God loves us enough to do just that. But there is also no doubt that his love is great enough to love a whole universe full of life.

My personal opinion is that God created the universe fairly teeming with life. If even one star carries one life-giving planet per galaxy, there are still billions of galaxies and thus billions of such planets are possible. My guess is that even our galaxy has fellow travelers silently orbiting stars like the sun that spiral around the black hole at the galaxy center. Ever since science began to challenge the geocentric concept of the universe revealing the enormity of the heavens and our relative unimportance in the physical universe, our status and our self-centered egos have taken a beating. Always we have fallen toward lesser importance. I don't think this will change as we explore the universe further. Instead, we will find that we are only one among many. Perhaps then, we on earth will realize that our common heritage binds us together as a single species, a brotherhood by creation, a brotherhood in blood, as Jesus proclaimed. Let us pray that we might learn that lesson before it is forced upon us by someone from somewhere else.

By now our first television broadcasts have reached the region of our nearest stellar neighbors. The nearest star is Alpha Centauri, about 4.3 light-years away. The star Vega is only twenty-six light-years away (a light-year is the distance that light or radio/TV waves will travel in one year, almost six trillion miles), so Vegans can now tune in on TV from the seventies—if there are Vegans. There are about 10,000 stars less than 100 light-years away. Since most of the stars we can see with the naked eye are less than a few hundred light-years away, it won't be very long before they will know we are here. If life is abundant in the galaxy, it may not be long before our television waves do reach a planet with intelligent life capable of intercepting and interpreting them. What a picture of us they will reveal. The late Carl Sagan, in his delightful novel, *Contact*, about the first contact with extraterrestrials, imagines that Vegans had detected even the faint television images broadcast of Hitler opening the 1936 Olympic games. (Radio waves are bent by the atmosphere and don't escape into space as easily, while the waves used for television are not bent and can escape.)

The odds, however, are very great that advanced intelligence may be so far away that those television signals will be too weak when they get there to be detected among all the naturally occurring radio noise of the universe. We have not detected any extraterrestrial TV transmissions, and presumably other civilizations would have passed this immature stage long ago.

But we want to know now if someone is out there. We don't want to wait several generations, or even one. As a result, radioastronomers today are conducting sky surveys to try to detect transmissions from anyone intelligent and advanced enough to be seeking us among the stars. The rationale is, if there is a multitude of planets with intelligent life, there must be many as advanced as we are, and probably many who are much more technically advanced than we. These beings will, presumably, be asking the same questions we are asking and seeking to know if there is anyone else out there. To this date there has been no hint of a rational signal observed. But the SETI (Search for Extraterrestrial Intelligence) searchers are quick to point out that only a part of the sky has been covered. With the newest computer techniques, we are finally capable of making a real effort to cover the vastness of the space around us.

Reports continually appear in the news about UFO sightings. For years we have been hearing fantastic tales about mysterious flying saucers and cigar-shaped objects with flashing lights seen by airplanes in flight and strange lights harassing cars driven on lonely roads. Some people, quite seriously claim to have been abducted by extraterrestrials and examined on their spaceships. What are as Christians to make of all this? Is it nonsense, the working of overactive imaginations, or the need for some unimportant people to get attention? Is it real, yet so ultimately shattering to our culture and society that the information is being suppressed? The scientific approach is undoubtedly the best in such situations. Only documented proof will suffice to satisfy scientists that these events are really true. Personally, I try to be open-minded, but I will require more proof than I have now.

You see, there is a serious problem with interstellar communication that may preclude any physical interaction between intelligence on different planetary systems. Since our space probes within our own solar system have shown eight probably sterile planets, interesting but empty of intelligent life, we are forced to try to communicate with intelligence living on planets in some other star system. These systems, even the closest, are five light years away. Albert Einstein in his brilliant theory of relativity has shown that light is the fastest speed allowed to anything in the physical universe. It also is the speed of electricity and radio waves, 186,282 miles per second. Even to talk with someone five light-years away will take five years to send a message and five years to get a reply back. It will be extremely difficult to carry on a conversation with that time lag. And most stars having planets are probably much farther away. No interstellar gossip lines for sure.

The Interstellar Travel Problem

If interstellar conversation is a problem even when we can communicate at the speed of light, interstellar transportation is a more serious problem. Our fastest speed for a spacecraft is still in the thousands-of-miles-per-hour range. It has taken nearly a decade for our space probes to get to the relatively close outer regions of our solar system. *Pioneer*, launched in the seventies, is billions of miles from Earth, but is still detecting the presence of particles from the sun. Again, the problem is in the vast distances involved. The distances to the stars are so vast that the human mind can't conceive of them, so they are measured in light-years. Unless we can travel at the speed of light, there is little hope for interstellar travel, in spite of what science fiction leads us to believe.

To put this in perspective, consider that the moon, to which man has already traveled, is 240,000 miles from Earth. This is the closest astronomical object, and it is thirty earth diameters from us, much farther than most artist drawings place it. If the earth is drawn an inch in diameter, the moon must be drawn thirty inches away, and if the earth is only $1/8^{th}$ inch in diameter, the sun (93,000,000 miles away) must be drawn 120 feet away to be on scale. Thus, it is virtually impossible to draw a scale model of all the planets in their orbits around the sun on a practical-sized sheet of paper and have the earth big enough to be visible.

Einstein has shown that another problem occurs when and if we can travel near light speed. Time slows down, being itself relative to the speed you are traveling through space. This would be fine for the space traveler who makes the voyage because he would age only a few years on a one-hundred-year round-trip journey. But who wants to return to a wife and kids back on Earth who have aged one hundred years while you were gone? Who knows if the people who sent you will even be alive, or whether there will be anyone around who knows why you left one hundred years before? And that is to a relatively near star system which may not have any living planets around it, let alone planets harboring intelligent life. To travel to the center of our galaxy thirty thousand light years away would age the travelers four years traveling at the speed of light, but sixty thousand years would have passed on Earth. The people back on Earth would not know anything about you when you returned, assuming people were still here. That long ago, humans were still cave-dwellers. It could be that sixty thousand years from now, some new ultra-speed would be developed that could have sent people on your journey and back several times before you returned from the first.

If some intelligent being out there has found some way to overcome the limit of the speed of light, he will be far advanced over us and that could lead to disaster. If earth experience is any indication, the interaction of advanced technology with more primitive technology usually is bad for the primitive people. Let us pray, if this happens, that they are not only smarter, but also wiser and closer to the mind of God than we are. I think, however, that God in his wisdom created the light-speed limit and the vast distances to prevent that from happening. Our isolation may not be a curse but a haven. It may also prove to be protection for the other beings in the rest of the universe—from us.

Nowhere Else to Go

Our isolation further reinforces the imperative that we learn to live together on this planet as a unique form of intelligent life, possibly forever tied to this sphere of blue, our only refuge in a hostile physical universe. We must keep it fit for life, for all living things, and to do this, we must use our best science and technology and use it wisely. We have no place else to go out there. This is all there is, unless we want to live in space suits or glass bubbles on some cold barren sphere. It is inconceivable that such an existence could last very long, considering that we are unable to live as God planned here on Earth. This planet, our cradle, has a relatively benign environment because we were fitted to it exactly by evolution. To nowhere else in the universe will we be so well adapted. Earth is the planet God has given us, and we can't plan to shed it when we have ruined it, hoping to find another. Besides, any other planet so benign would probably have inhabitants that would not welcome our intrusion, especially with our dismal record. Our only escape from this planet is into the spiritual universe, which by God's grace is friendly and accepting to us—if we accept its open arms on God's terms not ours.

The discussion of intelligent beings somewhere else in the universe brings up the question of whether they also know God. Did he send his son to save them too? Or are they atheistic, evil creatures, sadistic and cruel? I think that the answer to that must be as it is on Earth. Societies will not function long without love and trust and truth. Hitler's thousand-year Reich lasted less than a decade by trying to thrive on terror and death. The Soviet Union lasted sixty years and couldn't keep up with the democratic world. We find again and again that even if governments attempt to live by lies and hatred, the common people do not stop loving their families, friends, neighbors, and God. The discovery that Christians have remained faithful, if unchurched, through years of repression and persecution in China is further evidence of the power of the spiritual universe in our lives.

As Christians, we believe that God is the creator of the universe, and he is God of the Vegans, the Polarians, the Altairians, and the Arcturians, as well as us Solarians on Earth. If they are wiser than we are, they should know him better than we do, if in entirely different ways. For I am convinced that if chemistry is chemistry throughout the universe, love must be love from star to star, from galaxy to galaxy the same.

Our Other Dwelling Places

There is another possible reason for the immensity of the universe. When Jesus said in John 14:02,

> In my Father's house there are many dwelling places; if it were not so, would I have told you that I go to prepare a place for you?(NRSV)

he may have been talking about the many planets that God our Father has created for us to live on. It is a possibility that we are reincarnated on another planet, in this galaxy or another, to live a physical life again. What it may mean is that when we ask the question, "Is anyone out there?" the answer comes back that WE are out there.

The only awareness of our physical lives may occur during the spiritual phases of our lives, and each incarnation may be a period for spiritual growth. This might seem abhorrent to Christians who are satisfied that this life has enough of suffering and struggle—

who are looking forward to being eternally with Jesus. Frankly, although being with Jesus must be wonderful, it sounds a rather monotonous role to have for eternity. Many theologians have despaired of heaven if it consists of floating around on clouds, playing harps, or just eternally singing praise to God. If the physical universe is dynamic and exciting, full of beauty and challenge, will the spiritual universe be any less so? Those characteristics of our human minds that rise above our animal nature are probably spiritual universe characteristics, more exquisitely experienced in that realm than we can ever know them in our limited existence here.

> For now we see in a mirror dimly, but then we shall see face to face. (1 Corinthians 13:12)(NRSV).

Our current life may be just one of many lives throughout eternity, if we seek to recognize and respond to the God of the universe.

Leslie Weatherhead pointed out in Matthew 17:12-13 that Jesus said Elijah had come, and the disciples understood this to mean John the Baptist. Jesus didn't deny the occurrence of reincarnation, missing a great opportunity to correct a common error in the belief of the day—if it was an error. That of course, is a negative proof, which proves nothing. Most Christians believe that Jesus is an incarnation of a pre-existing spirit, which may mean that pre-existing spirits can become flesh and blood at least once. In Jeremiah, God says

> Before I formed you in the womb I knew you. (Jeremiah 1:5)(NRSV)

This implies a previous existence. The concept of reincarnation on this earth has been the fascinating subject of many books and even television programs. Remarkably, this is never conducted in a Christian context, probably because the church has taught against reincarnation. It is a mystery. I try to be open to the concept for it makes some logical sense, all the while certain that knowing God in Jesus Christ is what really matters.

To carry the implications of reincarnation further, one could deduce that our fate, our hell, for not accepting the gift of God's grace, is to forever recycle our existence on earth until we get it right as the Hindus believe. Or get exiled to a fiery planet hell as one of my pastors suggested. By contrast, our gift of spiritual life as a child of God may give us the right to live throughout the entire universe—to experience the fantastic other worlds God has created—worlds with two suns and myriad moons, with a brilliant galaxy gleaming just overhead at night, or with crystal mountains beneath a sky resplendent with rainbow colored rings. All this there might be, but more beautiful still is to know our God more closely and to serve him more dearly on whatever world we live.

I realize this is totally fanciful and rather unorthodox Christianity at that. There is a delicious mystery about our faith in God and Jesus Christ. Science has removed a portion of the mystery of the physical world, only to uncover infinitely more unknowns. Jesus has revealed much of the mystery of the spiritual world, only to suggest infinitely more. But that is good, for without mystery life would not be nearly so delicious.

What God has planned for us beyond our life on earth is in his loving hands. We only know it will be marvelous and that nothing can separate us from his love. As Paul wrote in Romans 8:38-39,

> For I am convinced that neither death, nor life, nor angels,
> nor rulers, nor things present, nor things to come, nor powers,
> nor height, nor depth, nor anything else in all creation, will
> be able to separate us from the love of God in Christ Jesus
> our Lord. (NRSV)

I know not what the future hath
Of marvel or surprise,
Assured alone that life and death
God's mercy underlies.

And if my heart and flesh are weak
To bear an untried pain,
The bruised reed he will not break,
But strengthen and sustain.

And thou, O Lord, by whom are seen
They creatures as they be,
Forgive me if too close I lean
My human heart to thee.

And so beside the silent sea
I wait the muffled oar;
No harm from him can come to me
On ocean or on shore.

I know not where his islands lift
Their fronded palms in air;
I only know I cannot drift
Beyond his love and care.

John Greenleaf Whittier

THE LAST WORD

I hope you have enjoyed our little trip through science and faith, as much as I have enjoyed writing it. I have tried to show that the truth of science and the truth of faith are not incompatible as some would have us believe. It does no service to God and certainly none to the Christian faith or to the Bible to misrepresent life so badly.

My purpose has not been to justify science, however, but to build faith. I firmly believe that by basing our view of our physical life on facts and reality rather than mythology and misrepresentation, we will build our house of faith on rock not sand. No new scientific discovery, no interstellar traveler, no nuclear catastrophe, not even our own imminent death can then shake our faith in God, for we have put our physical existence into its proper place.

As long as the physical world is our home, we are here to serve God by serving our fellow man. We must base our life here on the facts of the physical universe if we are to do that well. Science is a gift God has given us for that purpose. If we misuse that knowledge, it is our sin.

Yet we know that our ultimate home is in the spiritual universe. It is my prayer that you will see God's promise of citizenship in the spiritual universe as a goal worthy of a lifetime of devotion. If so, this book will have served its purpose.

May God bless you.

Eugene R. Wagner

BOOKS CITED

Abbott, Edwin A. *Flatland, A Romance of Many Dimensions.* New York: Dover Publications, 1992.

Batton, Mary. *Discovery by Chance, Science and the Unexpected.* New York: Funk and Wagnalls, 1968.

Dawkins, Richard. *The Blind Watchmaker.* New York: W.W. Norton and Company, 1986.

Davies, Paul. *Superforce.* New York: Simon and Schuster, 1984. *Quotations reprinted with the permission of Simon & Schuster Adult Publishing Group from SUPERFORCE by Paul Davies. Copyright © 1984 by Glenister Gavin Ltd.*

Drummond, Henry. *Natural Laws in the Spiritual World.* Philadelphia: Henry Altemus, 1892.

Good News Bible, Today's English Version. Nashville: Thomas Nelson Publishers, 1986. *Quotations used by permission of the American Bible Society*

Holy Bible, New International Version. Grand Rapids: Zondervan Bible Publishers, 1987. *Scripture taken from the HOLY BIBLE, NEW INTERNATIONAL VERSION. Copyright © 1973, 1978,* 1984 International Bible Society. Used by permission of Zondervan Bible Publishers.

The Holy Bible, New Revised Standard Version. Nashville: Thomas Nelson Publishers, 1989. *Scripture Quotations are from the New*

Revised Standard Version of the Bible, copyright © 1989 by the Division of Christian Education of the National Council of the Churches of Christ in the USA. Used by permission.

Kushner, Harold S. *When Bad Things Happen to Good People.* New York: Schocken Books. *Copyright © 1981 by Harold S. Kushner. Quotations used by permission of Schocken Books, a division of Random House, Inc.*

Morris, Desmond. *The Naked Ape.* New York: New Dell Publishing Company, 1969. Quotations used with permission.

Robinson, John. *Honest to God.* Philadelphia: The Westminster Press, 1963.

Sagan, Carl. *Contact.* New York: Simon and Schuster, 1985. *Quotation reprinted with the permission of Simon & Schuster Adult Publishing Group from CONTACT by Carl Sagan. Copyright ©1985, 1986, 1987 by Carl Sagan.*

Weatherhead, Leslie D. *The Christian Agnostic.* Nashville: Abingdon Press, 1965. *Quotations used by permission of Abingdon Press.*